Video BASICS Workbook

6

Herbert Zettl

San Francisco State University

WADSWORTH
CENGAGE Learning™

Australia • Brazil • Japan • Korea • Mexico • Singapore • Spain • United Kingdom • United States

Video Basics Workbook, Sixth Edition
Herbert Zettl

Senior Publisher: Lyn Uhl

Publisher: Michael Rosenberg

Development Editor: Ed Dodd

Assistant Editor: Megan Garvey

Editorial Assistant: Rebekah Matthews

Technology Project Manager: Jessica Badiner

Marketing Manager: Erin Mitchell

Marketing Coordinator: Darlene Macanan

Marketing Communications Manager:
    Christine Dobberpuhl

Senior Content Project Manager: Michael Lepera

Art Director: Linda Helcher

Print Buyer: Justin Palmeiro

Permissions Editor: Mardell Glinski Schultz

Production Service/Compositor:
    Gary Palmatier, Ideas to Images

Text Designer: Gary Palmatier, Ideas to Images

Photo Manager: Amanda Groszko

Photo Researcher: Catherine Schnurr,
    Pre-PressPMG

Copy Editor: Elizabeth von Radics

Cover Designer: Gary Palmatier, Ideas to Images

Cover Images: Edward Aiona (reporter, bicycle
    race) and Panasonic (camera)

For product information and technology assistance, contact us at
Cengage Learning Customer & Sales Support, 1-800-354-9706

For permission to use material from this text or product, submit all requests online at **www.cengage.com/permissions**. Further permissions questions can be e-mailed to **permissionrequest@cengage.com**.

ISBN-13: 978-0-495-57248-0
ISBN-10: 0-495-57248-9

Wadsworth
25 Thomson Place
Boston, MA 02210-1202
USA

Cengage Learning products are represented in Canada by Nelson Education, Ltd.

For your course and learning solutions, visit **academic.cengage.com**

Purchase any of our products at your local college store or at our preferred online store **www.ichapters.com**

Printed in Canada
1 2 3 4 5 6 7 12 11 10 09

Contents

Photo Credits

Edward Aiona: All photos not otherwise credited

Thomson Grass Valley: 103, 104, 105 (top), 106 (top)

Lowel-Light Mfg., Inc.: 82 (nos. 62, 65, 66, 67)

Mole-Richardson Co.: 82 (nos. 59, 61, 64)

Selco Products Company: 70 (ex. 5)

Herbert Zettl: 53 (ex. 3d), 55 (ex. 1a, 1c), 58 (ex. 6, 7), 82 (nos. 60, 63), 95 (no. 23), 145, 182 (ex. 1b)

Preface

Purpose   The primary objective of *Video Basics Workbook 6* is to reinforce students' learning and help them bridge as much as possible the gap between reading and doing. As a student of the basics of video production, you might be tempted to simply open the textbook and copy the readily available answers to the *Workbook* questions. But this will not speed up your learning process. What *will* facilitate learning is to answer the questions independent of the text. In this context the *Workbook* lets you practice retrieval of the knowledge you have acquired by reading the text. As you well know, the value of learning is not so much what you stuff into your head but what comes out of it on demand.

Instructors can use the *Workbook* as a convenient diagnostic tool—to find out not so much what students know but what they *don't* know or can't readily recall. This way you, the instructor, can spotlight certain production areas that need attention and assign appropriate field and studio production activities to make up for the deficiencies. The *Workbook* also provides you with an objective tool for assessing student comprehension of the language of video production, the basic production techniques, and how to apply certain techniques in a variety of production contexts.

Organization   This edition of the *Workbook* closely follows the chapter sequence of the *Video Basics 6* text. As in the main text, the unique characteristics and the production requirements of digital television are emphasized throughout the *Workbook*. Despite this close correlation, however, the *Workbook* chapters are self-contained and can be assigned independently and in any order desired.

Learning objectives   All the problems in the *Workbook* are structured with these specific learning objectives in mind:

■ *To reinforce the learning of video terminology, production tools, and production procedures and techniques.* The review of the key terms and the multiple-choice questions are to test students' knowledge of the terminology and the basic tools of video production—what they are and how they work. These exercises are to check student comprehension. If students have no trouble matching the key terms with their definitions and can answer the multiple-choice questions with relative ease without having to look up the answers in *Video Basics 6,* they have successfully learned the required material. The Problem-solving Applications will test whether students can apply the material in a variety of hypothetical production contexts. The final and most important criterion is of course whether students can apply the basic techniques in an actual video production.

- *To facilitate the retrieval of information when needed.* By completing the review sections without looking up any answers, students will quickly discover their strong and weak points. After pinpointing their strengths and weaknesses, they can go back to the text and, if available, to *Zettl's VideoLab 3.0* DVD-ROM and remedy their deficiencies.

- *To facilitate the efficient and effective application of video production equipment and practices.* The multiple-choice questions test students on what they should do—and how to do it—in various production situations. *Zettl's VideoLab 3.0* DVD-ROM offers students further opportunities to practice in the Try It and Quiz sections.

- *To find creative solutions to production problems.* As mentioned, the Problem-solving Applications challenge students to come up with creative solutions to common production problems. Note that the problem-solving section invites various answers, depending on the specific production context or available equipment. In solving these problems, students should, at least initially, not feel limited by budget and time restrictions. The floor plan and storyboard sheets are included to visualize sets, shots, and shot sequences and to make the format relatively uniform.

Acknowledgments   Once again, my first thanks go to the people at Wadsworth/ Cengage Learning who insisted on a workbook that is as efficient in its use as it is effective in student learning. My thanks go especially to Gary Palmatier of Ideas to Images for his transparent layout and clear illustrations and to Elizabeth von Radics for her precise editing; their contributions eliminated possible ambiguities and greatly assist students in achieving the learning objectives. As with the *Video Basics* text, Paul Rose of University of Utah deserves an additional thank-you for his suggestions about the *Workbook* content and for improving the multiple-choice questions.

I am also indebted to my colleagues at San Francisco State University and other institutions, and especially to my students, who helped me directly or indirectly by asking questions, by making mistakes I expected, and by finding solutions I did not expect.

Special thanks go to my wife, Erika, who as a longtime classroom teacher, administrator, and educational consultant helped me clarify the questions and objectify the answers without impinging on students' creativity.

Herbert Zettl

Production:
Processes and People

Production Process

REVIEW OF KEY TERMS

Match each term with its appropriate definition by filling in the corresponding bubble.

1. **program objective**
2. **medium requirements**
3. **single-camera production**

4. **preproduction**
5. **production**
6. **multicamera production**

7. **postproduction**
8. **angle**

A.   Production activities after the video-recording phase

A	① ② ③ ④
	1 2 3 4
	⑤ ⑥ ⑦ ⑧
	5 6 7 8

B.   The desired effect of a program on the viewer

B	① ② ③ ④
	1 2 3 4
	⑤ ⑥ ⑦ ⑧
	5 6 7 8

C.   The equipment, facilities, and people necessary for a specific production

C	① ② ③ ④
	1 2 3 4
	⑤ ⑥ ⑦ ⑧
	5 6 7 8

D.   The basic point of view that dominates the approach to a story

D	① ② ③ ④
	1 2 3 4
	⑤ ⑥ ⑦ ⑧
	5 6 7 8

PAGE TOTAL [ ]

1. program objective	4. preproduction	7. postproduction
2. medium requirements	5. production	8. angle
3. single-camera production	6. multicamera production	

E. Activities during the planning of a production

E ◯ ◯ ◯ ◯
  1 2 3 4
  ◯ ◯ ◯ ◯
  5 6 7 8

F. The use of several cameras for the simultaneous video recording of an event

F ◯ ◯ ◯ ◯
  1 2 3 4
  ◯ ◯ ◯ ◯
  5 6 7 8

G. A film-style approach to video recording

G ◯ ◯ ◯ ◯
  1 2 3 4
  ◯ ◯ ◯ ◯
  5 6 7 8

H. Activities during which the production is telecast live or recorded

H ◯ ◯ ◯ ◯
  1 2 3 4
  ◯ ◯ ◯ ◯
  5 6 7 8

PAGE TOTAL

SECTION TOTAL

REVIEW OF PRODUCTION MODEL

1. Identify each part of the production model diagram and fill in the bubbles with the corresponding numbers.

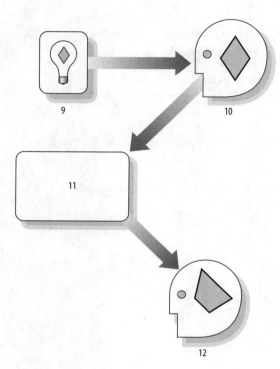

a. medium requirements

b. basic idea

c. message actually received

d. desired effect

1a ○ ○ ○ ○
    9   10   11   12

1b ○ ○ ○ ○
    9   10   11   12

1c ○ ○ ○ ○
    9   10   11   12

1d ○ ○ ○ ○
    9   10   11   12

PAGE TOTAL ☐

Select the correct answers and fill in the bubbles with the corresponding numbers.

2. The most important initial step in the production model is to (13) *determine the available production equipment* (14) *define the program objective* (15) *contact production personnel.*

3. The medium requirements include (16) *equipment but not program content and people* (17) *equipment and people* (18) *equipment, production elements, and people.*

4. The closer the actually received message is to the (19) *program objective* (20) *producer's objective* (21) *medium requirements,* the more successful the program.

5. The message that ultimately counts is the one that is (22) *carefully constructed by the producer* (23) *transmitted by the originating institution* (24) *received and interpreted by the viewer.*

6. Medium requirements are basically determined by (25) *the program objective* (26) *the chief engineer* (27) *the available equipment.*

7. The "angle" describes (28) *a critical view of the program objective* (29) *the basic approach to the production* (30) *the point of view of the audience.*

2	○ 13	○ 14	○ 15
3	○ 16	○ 17	○ 18
4	○ 19	○ 20	○ 21
5	○ 22	○ 23	○ 24
6	○ 25	○ 26	○ 27
7	○ 28	○ 29	○ 30

PAGE TOTAL

SECTION TOTAL

REVIEW OF PRODUCTION PROCESSES

Select the correct answers and fill in the bubbles with the corresponding numbers.

1. In the preproduction flowchart below, match each major step with the corresponding number.

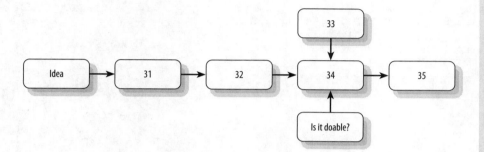

a. angle

b. script

c. Is it worth doing?

d. evaluation

e. program objective

	31	32	33	34	35
1a	○	○	○	○	○
1b	○	○	○	○	○
1c	○	○	○	○	○
1d	○	○	○	○	○
1e	○	○	○	○	○

PAGE TOTAL

2. In the preproduction flowchart below, match each major step with the corresponding number.

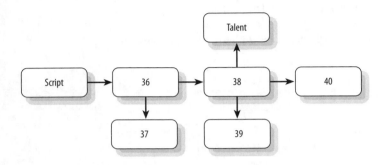

a. producer

b. art director

c. director

d. budget

e. facilities/equipment/tech personnel

2a ○ ○ ○ ○ ○
   36 37 38 39 40

2b ○ ○ ○ ○ ○
   36 37 38 39 40

2c ○ ○ ○ ○ ○
   36 37 38 39 40

2d ○ ○ ○ ○ ○
   36 37 38 39 40

2e ○ ○ ○ ○ ○
   36 37 38 39 40

PAGE
TOTAL

SECTION
TOTAL

REVIEW OF CONVERGENCE OF STUDIO AND FIELD PRODUCTION

1. Fill in the bubbles whose numbers correspond with the appropriate camera setup as shown in the diagrams below and on the following page.

   a. single-camera film-style

   b. multicamera switched

   c. multicamera iso

1a	○ 41	○ 42	○ 43
1b	○ 41	○ 42	○ 43
1c	○ 41	○ 42	○ 43

SECTION TOTAL

43

Event   Camcorder

Recording CU

Recording MS

Recording LS

Recording XLS

Postproduction editing

■ REVIEW QUIZ

*Mark the following statements as true or false by filling in the bubbles in the **T** (for true) or **F** (for false) column.*

		T	F
1.	The audience is largely irrelevant when establishing the program objective.	**1** ○ 44	○ 45
2.	Because production is primarily a creative activity, any type of production system would prove counterproductive.	**2** ○ 46	○ 47
3.	When brainstorming for new ideas, somebody should make sure that the ideas generated are always relevant to the topic.	**3** ○ 48	○ 49
4.	Medium requirements include production personnel, equipment, and facilities.	**4** ○ 50	○ 51
5.	The preproduction process includes the statement of the medium requirements.	**5** ○ 52	○ 53
6.	Successful brainstorming requires a discussion leader who prevents irrelevant ideas.	**6** ○ 54	○ 55
7.	The program objective is important for the preproduction phase and the production phase but not the postproduction phase.	**7** ○ 56	○ 57
8.	Clustering and brainstorming are similar idea-creating techniques.	**8** ○ 58	○ 59
9.	The signals of a multicamera setup can be fed into the switcher or into separate recorders for each camera.	**9** ○ 60	○ 61
10.	In the context of preproduction, an "angle" means a specific camera field of view.	**10** ○ 62	○ 63

SECTION TOTAL [ ]

PROBLEM-SOLVING APPLICATIONS

1. Do a brainstorming session. Have several people engaged in the same production problem sit in a circle, then place the mic of a small audiotape recorder in the center of the circle. Describe the general theme of the production, such as "improving education in this country" or "the importance of art in elementary schools." Do not try to state the general idea as a program objective. The specific program objective should develop out of the brainstorming session.

   A good way to begin is to have one of the group members say something neutral, such as "Knock-knock-who's there?" or "Hello, what can I do for you?" Make sure that *all* ideas are accepted and not commented on, however far-out or ridiculous they may be. During the playback you can be more discriminating and select only those ideas that fit your overall production theme. See whether, and how, this material might help you design a program objective and/or the medium translation of the objective.

2. Select a key word signifying your program theme and do an idea cluster. Use the cluster to develop the program objective, the specific program type (interview, documentary, drama), and the production approach (studio, ENG, EFP, single-camera, multicamera).

3. The producer who leads the brainstorming session for new show ideas says that she doesn't have to audio-record all the comments because she is writing down the relevant ones anyway. Do you agree with her?

4. In a follow-up session to define the program objective, the art director says not to worry about cameras, microphones, or even budgets right now but rather to focus on what the viewers should get out of the program. Do you agree with him? Be specific.

5. Expand the clusters indicated in the following three figures and develop a precise program objective from each.

2

Production Team: Who Does What When?

REVIEW OF KEY TERMS

Match each term with its appropriate definition by filling in the corresponding bubble.

1. **nontechnical production personnel**
2. **technical production personnel**
3. **production schedule**
4. **preproduction team**
5. **production team**
6. **EFP team**
7. **time line**
8. **postproduction team**

A. Category for crew members such as camera operators, floor persons, and audio engineers

A ○ ○ ○ ○
   1 2 3 4
   ○ ○ ○ ○
   5 6 7 8

B. A schedule that shows the time allotment for various activities during the production day

B ○ ○ ○ ○
   1 2 3 4
   ○ ○ ○ ○
   5 6 7 8

C. Consists of a variety of nontechnical and technical people, such as the producer and various assistants (associate producer and PA), the director and assistant, and the talent and production crew

C ○ ○ ○ ○
   1 2 3 4
   ○ ○ ○ ○
   5 6 7 8

D. Consists of director, video editor, and sometimes sound designer

D ○ ○ ○ ○
   1 2 3 4
   ○ ○ ○ ○
   5 6 7 8

PAGE TOTAL [ ]

1. nontechnical production personnel
2. technical production personnel
3. production schedule
4. preproduction team
5. production team
6. EFP team
7. time line
8. postproduction team

E. A calendar that lists major production activities

E   ① ② ③ ④
    1   2   3   4
    ⑤ ⑥ ⑦ ⑧
    5   6   7   8

F. Usually the talent, camcorder operator, and utility person

F   ① ② ③ ④
    1   2   3   4
    ⑤ ⑥ ⑦ ⑧
    5   6   7   8

G. Category for personnel such as producers, directors, and talent

G   ① ② ③ ④
    1   2   3   4
    ⑤ ⑥ ⑦ ⑧
    5   6   7   8

H. Consists of people who plan the production, normally including the producer, director, writer, art director, and technical supervisor or technical director; large productions may also include a composer and a choreographer

H   ① ② ③ ④
    1   2   3   4
    ⑤ ⑥ ⑦ ⑧
    5   6   7   8

PAGE TOTAL ☐

SECTION TOTAL ☐

REVIEW OF PRODUCTION PERSONNEL AND RESPONSIBILITIES

Identify the person mainly responsible for the following production situations and fill in the bubbles with the corresponding numbers.

1. Last-minute changes to the names on the final credits are made by the (9) *art director* (10) *TD* (11) *C.G. operator.*

   1 ○ 9   ○ 10   ○ 11

2. Making sure that the dancers can hear the music recording is the responsibility of the (12) *LD* (13) *AD* (14) *audio engineer.*

   2 ○ 12   ○ 13   ○ 14

3. The talent wants to make sure that he can see the opening cues. He should talk to the (15) *director* (16) *producer* (17) *floor manager.*

   3 ○ 15   ○ 16   ○ 17

4. Informing talent and crew about a production schedule change is the responsibility of the (18) *floor manager* (19) *producer* (20) *TD.*

   4 ○ 18   ○ 19   ○ 20

5. Arranging various shots in postproduction is done by the (21) *producer* (22) *video operator* (23) *editor.*

   5 ○ 21   ○ 22   ○ 23

6. The person in charge of camera rehearsals is the (24) *director* (25) *AD* (26) *TD.*

   6 ○ 24   ○ 25   ○ 26

7. Having the scenery set up and the set decorated by the scheduled time is the responsibility of the (27) *floor manager* (28) *director* (29) *TD.*

   7 ○ 27   ○ 28   ○ 29

8. The time line is done by the (30) *floor manager* (31) *director* (32) *art director.*

   8 ○ 30   ○ 31   ○ 32

9. To increase the overall light level in a scene, you should ask the (33) *LD* (34) *PA* (35) *floor manager.*

   9 ○ 33   ○ 34   ○ 35

10. The producer complains about the "static look" of the set. To correct the situation, she must talk to the (36) *TD* (37) *art director* (38) *executive producer.*

    10 ○ 36   ○ 37   ○ 38

SECTION TOTAL [   ]

*From the list below, select the major items omitted from the following time line and fill in the corresponding bubbles. **Note: This list contains items that are not part of the customary time line.***

Time Line: April 15 — Panel Discussion (Studio 1)

8:30–9:00 a.m.	Tech meeting
9:00–11:00 a.m.	Setup and lighting
12:00–12:15 p.m.	Notes and reset
12:15–12:30 p.m.	Briefing of panel guests
12:30–12:45 p.m.	Run-through and camera rehearsal
12:45–12:55 p.m.	Notes and reset
12:55–2:55 p.m.	Recording
2:55–3:30 p.m.	Spill

(39) *tech meeting*

(40) *recording*

(41) *crew call*

(42) *notes*

(43) *strike*

(44) *camera rehearsal*

(45) *break*

(46) *lighting*

(47) *reset*

(48) *meal*

(49) *budget meeting*

(50) *preproduction meeting*

○ ○ ○ ○
39 40 41 42

○ ○ ○ ○
43 44 45 46

○ ○ ○ ○
47 48 49 50

SECTION TOTAL ☐

REVIEW QUIZ

*Mark the following statements as true or false by filling in the bubbles in the **T** (for true) or **F** (for false) column.*

		T	F
1.	Normally, the TD runs the video recorder.	**1** ○ 51	○ 52
2.	The editor is part of the preproduction team.	**2** ○ 53	○ 54
3.	Talent includes actors and performers.	**3** ○ 55	○ 56
4.	The audio engineer works the audio console during a show.	**4** ○ 57	○ 58
5.	The PA is usually responsible for notes.	**5** ○ 59	○ 60
6.	The AD is involved in preproduction but not in production.	**6** ○ 61	○ 62
7.	Principal camera positions and talent blocking are determined by the director.	**7** ○ 63	○ 64
8.	The director should have some influence on postproduction editing.	**8** ○ 65	○ 66
9.	The art director is responsible for putting up the studio set.	**9** ○ 67	○ 68
10.	The executive producer is always part of the field survey team.	**10** ○ 69	○ 70
11.	The LD is in charge of directing the log entries.	**11** ○ 71	○ 72
12.	The floor manager is principally responsible for the budget.	**12** ○ 73	○ 74

SECTION TOTAL [ ]

PROBLEM-SOLVING APPLICATIONS

1. The camera operators for a weekly two-camera interview series tell you, the producer, that they do not need a director because they have done the show many times and know every shot by heart. Do you agree? If so, why? If not, why not?

2. The ENG/EFP camcorder operator of a weekly on-location interview show tells you, the producer, that he does not need a director because he has done the show many times and knows what shots are required. Do you agree? If so, why? If not, why not?

3. The PA complains that the producer, the director, and even the floor manager ask her to write down specific production problems. Her comment is that, as a production assistant, she has to listen only to the producer. Is her complaint justified?

4. The talent complains to the director about the long hours and the relatively low pay. Is the talent complaining to the right person? If so, why? If not, to whom should the talent direct the complaints?

5. The novice director tells you, the AD, not to worry about the time line because he will move on to the next time block only when satisfied with rehearsing the current scene. Do you agree with him? If so, why? If not, why not?

Image Creation:
Digital Video and Camera

Image Formation and Digital Video

REVIEW OF KEY TERMS

Match each term with its appropriate definition by filling in the corresponding bubble.

1. 720p
2. 1080i
3. analog
4. digital
5. compression

6. sampling
7. codec
8. HDV
9. HDTV
10. interlaced scanning

11. progressive scanning
12. field
13. frame
14. quantizing
15. refresh rate

A. A recording system that produces the same resolution as HDTV but which is more compressed than HDTV

B. The scanning cycle of all odd or even lines

C. A complete scanning cycle of the electron beam

PAGE TOTAL

23

1. 720p	6. sampling	11. progressive scanning
2. 1080i	7. codec	12. field
3. analog	8. HDV	13. frame
4. digital	9. HDTV	14. quantizing
5. compression	10. interlaced scanning	15. refresh rate

D. A signal that fluctuates like the original stimulus

D ○1 ○2 ○3 ○4 ○5 ○6 ○7 ○8 ○9 ○10 ○11 ○12 ○13 ○14 ○15

E. The system that scans all odd-numbered lines and then all even-numbered lines

E ○1 ○2 ○3 ○4 ○5 ○6 ○7 ○8 ○9 ○10 ○11 ○12 ○13 ○14 ○15

F. The scanning system that consists of two 540-line fields (some claim that there are two 539½-line fields)

F ○1 ○2 ○3 ○4 ○5 ○6 ○7 ○8 ○9 ○10 ○11 ○12 ○13 ○14 ○15

G. A step in the digitizing of an analog signal; it changes the sampling points into discrete values

G ○1 ○2 ○3 ○4 ○5 ○6 ○7 ○8 ○9 ○10 ○11 ○12 ○13 ○14 ○15

H. Can be one of several compression systems of digital video, graphics, and audio files

H ○1 ○2 ○3 ○4 ○5 ○6 ○7 ○8 ○9 ○10 ○11 ○12 ○13 ○14 ○15

PAGE TOTAL

I. High-definition television

I					
	○ 1	○ 2	○ 3	○ 4	○ 5
	○ 6	○ 7	○ 8	○ 9	○ 10
	○ 11	○ 12	○ 13	○ 14	○ 15

J. Selecting a great number of small parts of the analog signal at equally spaced intervals

J					
	○ 1	○ 2	○ 3	○ 4	○ 5
	○ 6	○ 7	○ 8	○ 9	○ 10
	○ 11	○ 12	○ 13	○ 14	○ 15

K. The consecutive scanning from top to bottom

K					
	○ 1	○ 2	○ 3	○ 4	○ 5
	○ 6	○ 7	○ 8	○ 9	○ 10
	○ 11	○ 12	○ 13	○ 14	○ 15

L. One of the accepted progressive scanning systems of DTV

L					
	○ 1	○ 2	○ 3	○ 4	○ 5
	○ 6	○ 7	○ 8	○ 9	○ 10
	○ 11	○ 12	○ 13	○ 14	○ 15

M. The number of complete scanning cycles per second

M					
	○ 1	○ 2	○ 3	○ 4	○ 5
	○ 6	○ 7	○ 8	○ 9	○ 10
	○ 11	○ 12	○ 13	○ 14	○ 15

N. Data in an on/off configuration

N					
	○ 1	○ 2	○ 3	○ 4	○ 5
	○ 6	○ 7	○ 8	○ 9	○ 10
	○ 11	○ 12	○ 13	○ 14	○ 15

PAGE TOTAL [   ]

1. 720p	6. sampling	11. progressive scanning
2. 1080i	7. codec	12. field
3. analog	8. HDV	13. frame
4. digital	9. HDTV	14. quantizing
5. compression	10. interlaced scanning	15. refresh rate

O. The temporary rearrangement or elimination of redundant picture information for more-efficient storage and signal transport

O   ○ ○ ○ ○ ○
    1 2 3 4 5
    ○ ○ ○ ○ ○
    6 7 8 9 10
    ○ ○ ○ ○ ○
    11 12 13 14 15

PAGE TOTAL

SECTION TOTAL

REVIEW OF BASIC IMAGE FORMATION

Select the correct answers and fill in the bubbles with the corresponding numbers.

1. An interlaced television frame consists of (16) *four fields* (17) *two fields* (18) *three fields*.

   1 ◯ 16   ◯ 17   ◯ 18

2. Each scanning line is made up of (19) *pixels* (20) *digits* (21) *numbers*.

   2 ◯ 19   ◯ 20   ◯ 21

3. To produce a complete frame in the 720p system, you need to scan (22) *720 lines* (23) *2 fields* (24) *1,440 fields*.

   3 ◯ 22   ◯ 23   ◯ 24

4. To produce a color image, a television receiver needs (25) *one* (26) *two* (27) *three* color signals.

   4 ◯ 25   ◯ 26   ◯ 27

5. In progressive scanning (28) *only the odd-numbered lines are scanned* (29) *only the even-numbered lines are scanned* (30) *each line is scanned from top to bottom in sequence*.

   5 ◯ 28   ◯ 29   ◯ 30

6. The 1080i system can use (31) *only interlaced scanning* (32) *only progressive scanning* (33) *either interlaced or progressive scanning*.

   6 ◯ 31   ◯ 32   ◯ 33

7. In progressive scanning each scanning cycle produces a (34) *field* (35) *frame*.

   7 ◯ 34   ◯ 35

8. In the 1080i system, you need (36) *2* (37) *1,080* (38) *540* fields to complete each frame.

   8 ◯ 36   ◯ 37   ◯ 38

SECTION TOTAL [ ]

REVIEW OF ANALOG AND DIGITAL PROCESSES

Select the correct answers and fill in the bubbles with the corresponding numbers.

1. A digital signal operates on the (39) *on/off* (40) *continuous wave* (41) *sine wave* principle.

1 ○ ○ ○
    39   40   41

2. Which of the two sampling rates shown below will produce the higher-quality signal?

2 ○ ○
    42   43

42   43

3. The compression system that eliminates redundant digital information is called (44) *low-sampling* (45) *lossy* (46) *high-sampling.*

3 ○ ○ ○
    44   45   46

4. One of the chief advantages of a digital over an analog video signal is that the digital signal (47) *can be dubbed many times without noticeable deterioration* (48) *can be sampled* (49) *can be interlaced.*

4 ○ ○ ○
    47   48   49

5. The compression system that compares frames for redundant information is called (50) *JPEG-3* (51) *MPEG-2* (52) *CODEC-4.*

5 ○ ○ ○
    50   51   52

6. The binary on/off code is normally represented by (53) *0's and 1's* (54) *1's and 2's* (55) *0's and 00's.*

6 ○ ○ ○
    53   54   55

7. When digitizing for high quality, the sampling rate should be (56) *as high as possible* (57) *as low as possible* (58) *neither because sampling is not a digitizing step.*

7 ○ ○ ○
    56   57   58

SECTION TOTAL [ ]

REVIEW QUIZ

*Mark the following statements as true or false by filling in the bubbles in the **T** (for true) or **F** (for false) column.*

		T	F
1.	An analog signal has a higher sampling rate than a digital one.	**1** ○ 59	○ 60
2.	In progressive scanning, each line is scanned consecutively from top to bottom.	**2** ○ 61	○ 62
3.	In interlaced scanning, two fields make up a complete frame.	**3** ○ 63	○ 64
4.	MPEG-2 is a lossy compression system.	**4** ○ 65	○ 66
5.	In interlaced scanning, each scanning cycle from top to bottom generates a frame.	**5** ○ 67	○ 68
6.	In progressive scanning, four fields make up a complete frame.	**6** ○ 69	○ 70
7.	In a digital system, the *on* state is usually represented by a 1, the *off* state by a 0.	**7** ○ 71	○ 72
8.	HDV is identical to HDTV.	**8** ○ 73	○ 74
9.	The 720p scanning system produces a complete frame at each scanning cycle.	**9** ○ 75	○ 76
10.	In progressive scanning, each scanning cycle from top to bottom generates a field.	**10** ○ 77	○ 78
11.	Similar to digital signals, analog signals can have lossy or lossless states of compression.	**11** ○ 79	○ 80
12.	The digital signal fluctuates exactly like the original stimulus.	**12** ○ 81	○ 82
13.	A digital signal can be compressed with various codecs.	**13** ○ 83	○ 84
14.	An analog signal can be compressed with MPEG-2 as well as JPEG codecs.	**14** ○ 85	○ 86
15.	Lossy compression is rarely used because it always leads to noticeable picture deterioration.	**15** ○ 87	○ 88

SECTION TOTAL [   ]

PROBLEM-SOLVING APPLICATIONS

1. You are asked to explain why, in most cases, we prefer digital over analog systems in video production. What is your response?

2. Demonstrate the relationship of sampling rate to signal fidelity. What graphics can you use to illustrate the principle of sampling?

3. You are asked to explain the basic difference between interlaced and progressive scanning. What are the advantages and the disadvantages of each system?

4. Why do we have different codecs, and what are their functions?

5. Why do we bother with sampling an analog signal that is already more complete than even the highest sampling rate can provide?

Course No. _____   Date _____   Name _____

4 Video Camera

REVIEW OF KEY TERMS

Match each term with its appropriate definition by filling in the corresponding bubble.

1. camera chain
2. camcorder
3. CCD
4. slow lens
5. CCU
6. fast lens
7. chrominance channel
8. aperture
9. focal length
10. zoom range
11. *f*-stop
12. beam splitter

A. The camera connected with the CCU, power supply, and sync generator

B. An electronic "chip"; it is the most common imaging device in color cameras

C. The iris opening of a lens

A   ① ② ③ ④ 1 2 3 4
    ⑤ ⑥ ⑦ ⑧ 5 6 7 8
    ⑨ ⑩ ⑪ ⑫ 9 10 11 12

B   ① ② ③ ④ 1 2 3 4
    ⑤ ⑥ ⑦ ⑧ 5 6 7 8
    ⑨ ⑩ ⑪ ⑫ 9 10 11 12

C   ① ② ③ ④ 1 2 3 4
    ⑤ ⑥ ⑦ ⑧ 5 6 7 8
    ⑨ ⑩ ⑪ ⑫ 9 10 11 12

PAGE TOTAL _____

1.	camera chain	5.	CCU	9.	focal length
2.	camcorder	6.	fast lens	10.	zoom range
3.	CCD	7.	chrominance channel	11.	*f*-stop
4.	slow lens	8.	aperture	12.	beam splitter

D. A lens that permits a relatively great amount of light to pass through at its largest aperture setting

D
○ ○ ○ ○
1 2 3 4
○ ○ ○ ○
5 6 7 8
○ ○ ○ ○
9 10 11 12

E. Contains the RGB video signals or some combination thereof

E
○ ○ ○ ○
1 2 3 4
○ ○ ○ ○
5 6 7 8
○ ○ ○ ○
9 10 11 12

F. The calibration on the lens indicating the aperture (and therefore the amount of light passing through the lens)

F
○ ○ ○ ○
1 2 3 4
○ ○ ○ ○
5 6 7 8
○ ○ ○ ○
9 10 11 12

G. Allows the VO to adjust the color and brightness balance before and during the production

G
○ ○ ○ ○
1 2 3 4
○ ○ ○ ○
5 6 7 8
○ ○ ○ ○
9 10 11 12

H. A portable camera with the VR attached to it to form a single, independent unit

H
○ ○ ○ ○
1 2 3 4
○ ○ ○ ○
5 6 7 8
○ ○ ○ ○
9 10 11 12

P A G E
T O T A L

I. Optical device within the camera that divides the white light into three primary colors: red, green, and blue

I
○ ○ ○ ○
1 2 3 4
○ ○ ○ ○
5 6 7 8
○ ○ ○ ○
9 10 11 12

J. A lens that permits a relatively small amount of light to pass through at its largest aperture

J
○ ○ ○ ○
1 2 3 4
○ ○ ○ ○
5 6 7 8
○ ○ ○ ○
9 10 11 12

K. Indicates how much of a scene the lens can see and how magnified the distant object looks

K
○ ○ ○ ○
1 2 3 4
○ ○ ○ ○
5 6 7 8
○ ○ ○ ○
9 10 11 12

L. The degree to which the focal length can be changed from a wide shot to a close-up during a zoom

L
○ ○ ○ ○
1 2 3 4
○ ○ ○ ○
5 6 7 8
○ ○ ○ ○
9 10 11 12

PAGE TOTAL ☐

SECTION TOTAL ☐

REVIEW OF CAMERA FUNCTION AND ELEMENTS

Select the correct answers and fill in the bubbles with the corresponding numbers.

1. The basic parts of the video camera are (13) *pedestal* (14) *lens* (15) *VR* (16) *imaging device* (17) *viewfinder* (18) *tally light.* (**Fill in three bubbles.**)

1 ◯ 13   ◯ 14   ◯ 15
  ◯ 16   ◯ 17   ◯ 18

2. Fill in the bubbles whose numbers correspond with the camera elements shown in the following figure.

a. transforms light into electric energy or video signals

b. amplifies video signals

c. processes video signal

d. converts video signals back into visible screen images

e. gathers and transmits the light

f. reflects light

g. splits the white light into red, green, and blue light beams

2a ◯ 19 ◯ 20 ◯ 21 ◯ 22
   ◯ 23 ◯ 24 ◯ 25

2b ◯ 19 ◯ 20 ◯ 21 ◯ 22
   ◯ 23 ◯ 24 ◯ 25

2c ◯ 19 ◯ 20 ◯ 21 ◯ 22
   ◯ 23 ◯ 24 ◯ 25

2d ◯ 19 ◯ 20 ◯ 21 ◯ 22
   ◯ 23 ◯ 24 ◯ 25

2e ◯ 19 ◯ 20 ◯ 21 ◯ 22
   ◯ 23 ◯ 24 ◯ 25

2f ◯ 19 ◯ 20 ◯ 21 ◯ 22
   ◯ 23 ◯ 24 ◯ 25

2g ◯ 19 ◯ 20 ◯ 21 ◯ 22
   ◯ 23 ◯ 24 ◯ 25

SECTION TOTAL

REVIEW OF LENSES

Select the correct answers and fill in the bubbles with the corresponding numbers.

1. A zoom lens has a (26) *wide* (27) *normal* (28) *narrow* (29) *variable* focal length.

2. In the diagram below, select the most appropriate *f*-stop number for each of the four apertures (**a** through **d**) and fill in the bubbles with the corresponding number.

a.   (30) *f*/22   (31) *f*/5.6   (32) *f*1.4

b.   (33) *f*/1.4   (34) *f*/2.8   (35) *f*/16

c.   (36) *f*/1.4   (37) *f*/4   (38) *f*/16

d.   (39) *f*/1.4   (40) *f*/8   (41) *f*/22

3. A short-focal-length lens gives (42) *a wider view than* (43) *a closer view than* (44) *the same vista as* a long-focal-length lens.

4. When reaching the maximum digital zoom-in position, the picture gets progressively (45) *sharper* (46) *smaller* (47) *pixelized.*

SECTION TOTAL

REVIEW OF THE IMAGING DEVICE, SIGNAL PROCESSING, AND CAMERA CHAIN

Select the correct answers and fill in the bubbles with the corresponding numbers.

1. The more pixels a CCD imaging device contains, the (48) *sharper* (49) *brighter* (50) *more colorful* the resulting screen image will be.

2. The NTSC signal is a (51) *composite* (52) *component* (53) *complex* signal.

3. The luminance signal is a (54) *color* (55) *composite* (56) *black-and-white* signal.

4. To function properly, camcorders do not need a (57) *power supply* (58) *video recorder* (59) *cable that connects them to the CCU.*

5. The standard studio camera chain consists of (60) *power supply, sync generator, and CCD* (61) *camera head, power supply, sync generator, and CCU* (62) *CCU, CCD, and power supply.*

6. The beam splitter changes (63) *the incoming light into RGB light beams* (64) *the incoming light into an electrical signal* (65) *the incoming light into color and black-and-white signals.*

7. For video recording, digital cinema uses (66) *high-end HDTV camcorders* (67) *movie cameras with a small TV camera attached* (68) *HDV camcorders with a film magazine attached.*

8. Studio cameras are normally controlled by (69) *their internal automatic controls* (70) *an external CCU* (71) *an internal CCU.*

9. The recording media that digital cinema cameras cannot use is (72) *videotape* (73) *35mm film* (74) *a hard drive.*

1	○ 48	○ 49	○ 50
2	○ 51	○ 52	○ 53
3	○ 54	○ 55	○ 56
4	○ 57	○ 58	○ 59
5	○ 60	○ 61	○ 62
6	○ 63	○ 64	○ 65
7	○ 66	○ 67	○ 68
8	○ 69	○ 70	○ 71
9	○ 72	○ 73	○ 74

SECTION TOTAL

REVIEW QUIZ

*Mark the following statements as true or false by filling in the bubbles in the **T** (for true) or*
***F** (for false) column.*

		T	F
1.	Camcorders can come with or without a video-recording device.	○ 75	○ 76
2.	A CCD changes light into electric energy.	○ 77	○ 78
3.	The wide-angle position of the zoom lens provides a vista similar to that of a short-focal-length lens.	○ 79	○ 80
4.	The sync generator and the power supply fulfill similar functions.	○ 81	○ 82
5.	ENG/EFP cameras are the same as ENG/EFP camcorders.	○ 83	○ 84
6.	HDV camcorders can record in 720p or 1080i.	○ 85	○ 86
7.	A fast lens is judged by its minimum f-stop number.	○ 87	○ 88
8.	The ENG/EFP camera contains the major parts of the regular camera chain.	○ 89	○ 90
9.	The CCU performs camera setup and control functions but does not help with keeping in focus during a zoom.	○ 91	○ 92
10.	The lower the f-stop number, the larger the aperture.	○ 93	○ 94
11.	Some ENG/EFP cameras can be connected to an RCU.	○ 95	○ 96
12.	*Zoom range* refers to how fast you can zoom in or out.	○ 97	○ 98
13.	All video cables must have BNC connectors.	○ 99	○ 100
14.	Digital cinema cameras are high-end HDTV camcorders.	○ 101	○ 102
15.	A beam splitter divides the incoming white light into red, green, and blue light beams.	○ 103	○ 104

SECTION TOTAL [ ]

PROBLEM-SOLVING APPLICATIONS

1. The camera operator tells you not to worry about the bright white cap of the dark-skinned golf pro. He says that the automatic iris of the camcorder will take care of the proper exposure. What is your reaction?

2. The director of a multicamera field production is worried that the cameras might not deliver pictures whose colors match when edited together. The TD tells the director that the use of RCUs will greatly help in color matching. Do you agree with the TD?

3. The director tells you that for covering an outdoor sporting event, a lens with a great zoom range is more important than an extremely fast one. Why does the director think so?

4. The director of a multicamera studio show is worried about having one of the cameras pan from a very brightly lighted scene to a very dark one. The TD tells her not to worry because the VO will use the CCU to take care of such problems. Why was the director worried about this pan in the first place? What was the TD talking about, and do you agree with the TD?

5. The director of a remote sporting event asks the TD to change the studio camera lens to one with a higher zoom ratio. How, if at all, would you defend such a request?

6. The producer is amazed that the DP of a digital cinema shoot prefers to work with a black-and-white viewfinder. How, if at all, would you defend the DP's position?

7. A salesperson of a well-known lens manufacturer tell you that the quality of the lens is almost as important for high-resolution images as the image sensor. Would you "buy" her statement? Be specific.

5 Operating the Camera

REVIEW OF KEY TERMS

Match each term with its appropriate definition by filling in the corresponding bubble.

1. arc
2. dolly
3. cant
4. crane
5. truck

6. tongue
7. mounting head
8. tilt
9. pedestal
10. pan

11. white balance
12. calibrate the zoom lens
13. shutter speed
14. jib arm

A. A device that connects the camera to its support

A
○ ○ ○ ○ ○
1 2 3 4 5
○ ○ ○ ○ ○
6 7 8 9 10
○ ○ ○ ○
11 12 13 14

B. To move the camera in a slightly curved dolly or truck

B
○ ○ ○ ○ ○
1 2 3 4 5
○ ○ ○ ○ ○
6 7 8 9 10
○ ○ ○ ○
11 12 13 14

C. Small crane that can be operated by the camera operator

C
○ ○ ○ ○ ○
1 2 3 4 5
○ ○ ○ ○ ○
6 7 8 9 10
○ ○ ○ ○
11 12 13 14

PAGE
TOTAL [   ]

1. arc	6. tongue	11. white balance
2. dolly	7. mounting head	12. calibrate the zoom lens
3. cant	8. tilt	13. shutter speed
4. crane	9. pedestal	14. jib arm
5. truck	10. pan	

D. To move the boom with the camera from left to right or from right to left

D ○1 ○2 ○3 ○4 ○5
   ○6 ○7 ○8 ○9 ○10
   ○11 ○12 ○13 ○14

E. Horizontal turning of the camera

E ○1 ○2 ○3 ○4 ○5
   ○6 ○7 ○8 ○9 ○10
   ○11 ○12 ○13 ○14

F. The adjustment of the color channels in the camera to produce a white color in lighting of various color temperatures

F ○1 ○2 ○3 ○4 ○5
   ○6 ○7 ○8 ○9 ○10
   ○11 ○12 ○13 ○14

G. To point the camera up or down

G ○1 ○2 ○3 ○4 ○5
   ○6 ○7 ○8 ○9 ○10
   ○11 ○12 ○13 ○14

H. To preset a zoom lens to keep it in focus throughout the zoom

H ○1 ○2 ○3 ○4 ○5
   ○6 ○7 ○8 ○9 ○10
   ○11 ○12 ○13 ○14

PAGE TOTAL [ ]

I. To move the camera up or down with a studio camera mount

I	○ 1	○ 2	○ 3	○ 4	○ 5
	○ 6	○ 7	○ 8	○ 9	○ 10
	○ 11	○ 12	○ 13	○ 14	

J. To move the camera toward or away from the object

J	○ 1	○ 2	○ 3	○ 4	○ 5
	○ 6	○ 7	○ 8	○ 9	○ 10
	○ 11	○ 12	○ 13	○ 14	

K. To move the camera laterally by means of a mobile camera mount

K	○ 1	○ 2	○ 3	○ 4	○ 5
	○ 6	○ 7	○ 8	○ 9	○ 10
	○ 11	○ 12	○ 13	○ 14	

L. The higher it is set, the sharper a moving object will be

L	○ 1	○ 2	○ 3	○ 4	○ 5
	○ 6	○ 7	○ 8	○ 9	○ 10
	○ 11	○ 12	○ 13	○ 14	

M. To move the boom of the camera crane up or down

M	○ 1	○ 2	○ 3	○ 4	○ 5
	○ 6	○ 7	○ 8	○ 9	○ 10
	○ 11	○ 12	○ 13	○ 14	

N. Tilting the camera sideways

N	○ 1	○ 2	○ 3	○ 4	○ 5
	○ 6	○ 7	○ 8	○ 9	○ 10
	○ 11	○ 12	○ 13	○ 14	

PAGE TOTAL [   ]

SECTION TOTAL [   ]

REVIEW OF CAMERA MOUNTS

Select the correct answers and fill in the bubbles with the corresponding numbers.

1. A spreader (15) *keeps the tripod legs from spreading too far* (16) *helps spread the tripod legs as much as possible* (17) *maximizes the spread of the tripod legs.*

2. The quick-release plate (18) *facilitates the mounting of a camera on the mounting head* (19) *secures the dolly base to the tripod legs.*

3. Fill in the bubbles whose numbers correspond with the camera movements indicated in the following figure.

a. dolly

1 ○	○	○
15	16	17

2 ○	○	
18	19	

3a ○	○	○
20	21	22
○	○	○
23	24	25

**P A G E
T O T A L** [   ]

b. truck

3b ◯ ◯ ◯
   20 21 22
   ◯ ◯ ◯
   23 24 25

c. tilt

3c ◯ ◯ ◯
   20 21 22
   ◯ ◯ ◯
   23 24 25

d. pan

3d ◯ ◯ ◯
   20 21 22
   ◯ ◯ ◯
   23 24 25

e. pedestal

3e ◯ ◯ ◯
   20 21 22
   ◯ ◯ ◯
   23 24 25

f. arc

3f ◯ ◯ ◯
   20 21 22
   ◯ ◯ ◯
   23 24 25

4. For all normal camera moves, the studio pedestal is normally set for (26) *parallel* (27) *tricycle* (28) *freewheeling* steering.

4 ◯ ◯ ◯
  26 27 28

5. A mounting head's drag control is important (29) *only for heavy studio cameras* (30) *only for lightweight camcorders* (31) *for both studio cameras and camcorders.*

5 ◯ ◯ ◯
  29 30 31

6. To minimize the wiggles of a handheld or shoulder-mounted camcorder, you should have the camera lens (32) *zoomed out all the way (wide-angle position)* (33) *zoomed in all the way (narrow-angle position)* (34) *zoomed in halfway (normal-focal-length position).*

6 ◯ ◯ ◯
  32 33 34

7. In the following figure, the dolly wheels on this studio pedestal are set for (35) *parallel* (36) *tricycle* (37) *freewheeling* steering.

7 ◯ ◯ ◯
  35 36 37

PAGE
TOTAL   [   ]

SECTION
TOTAL   [   ]

REVIEW OF OPERATIONAL FEATURES

Select the correct answers and fill in the bubbles with the corresponding numbers.

1. Calibrating, or presetting, the zoom lens means (38) *adjusting the zoom lens so that it stays in focus throughout the zoom* (39) *setting the proper f-stop* (40) *adjusting the zoom range.*

   | 1 | ◯ 38 | ◯ 39 | ◯ 40 |

2. Proper calibration of the zoom lens requires that you (41) *zoom in* (42) *zoom out* and focus on the target object (43) *closest to* (44) *farthest from* the camera. **(Fill in two bubbles.)**

   | 2 | ◯ 41 | ◯ 42 | ◯ 43 | ◯ 44 |

3. It is easiest to keep the image in focus when you are zoomed (45) *all the way in* (46) *halfway in* (47) *all the way out.*

   | 3 | ◯ 45 | ◯ 46 | ◯ 47 |

4. To cant a shoulder-mounted camcorder, you must tilt it (48) *down* (49) *sideways* (50) *up.*

   | 4 | ◯ 48 | ◯ 49 | ◯ 50 |

5. When white-balancing an ENG/EFP camera for covering a school board meeting in the school's multipurpose room, you should white-balance the camera (51) *in the hallway before entering the room* (52) *with a special white-balancing light* (53) *in the light that actually illuminates the area where the school board members sit.*

   | 5 | ◯ 51 | ◯ 52 | ◯ 53 |

6. When a fast-moving object blurs, you need to (54) *increase the shutter speed* (55) *decrease the shutter speed* (56) *open the aperture.*

   | 6 | ◯ 54 | ◯ 55 | ◯ 56 |

7. When panning with a shoulder-mounted camcorder, you should point your knees in the direction of the (57) *beginning of the pan* (58) *middle of the pan* (59) *end of the pan.*

   | 7 | ◯ 57 | ◯ 58 | ◯ 59 |

8. The focus-assist feature facilitates (60) *auto-focus* (61) *manual focus* (62) *manual and auto-focus.*

   | 8 | ◯ 60 | ◯ 61 | ◯ 62 |

SECTION TOTAL [ ]

REVIEW QUIZ

*Mark the following statements as true or false by filling in the bubbles in the **T** (for true) or **F** (for false) column.*

		T	F

1. The quick-release plate ensures the quick attachment and removal of the mounting head to and from the tripod.
   1 ○ 63 ○ 64

2. The depth of field depends on the focal length of the lens, the lens aperture, and the distance from camera to object.
   2 ○ 65 ○ 66

3. To ensure optimal color fidelity and continuity, you need to white-balance every time the camera is moved from one lighting environment to the next.
   3 ○ 67 ○ 68

4. Calibrating the zoom lens is necessary for ENG/EFP cameras as well as for studio cameras.
   4 ○ 69 ○ 70

5. The jib arm and the camera crane can make the camera move in similar ways.
   5 ○ 71 ○ 72

6. To calibrate a zoom lens, you must first zoom in and focus on the target object.
   6 ○ 73 ○ 74

7. With a jib arm, you can boom, tongue, and pan the camera in a single motion.
   7 ○ 75 ○ 76

8. To tilt up means to raise the camera pedestal.
   8 ○ 77 ○ 78

9. HDV and HDTV cameras are easier to focus than standard digital camcorders.
   9 ○ 79 ○ 80

10. The automatic focus on a camcorder guarantees staying in focus at all times.
    10 ○ 81 ○ 82

11. The best way to lock the camera mounting head when leaving the camera unattended is to tighten the drag control.
    11 ○ 83 ○ 84

12. Dolly and truck movements show up as similar movements on the screen.
    12 ○ 85 ○ 86

13. Generally, tight close-ups have a shallow depth of field.
    13 ○ 87 ○ 88

14. To avoid blurring a fast-moving object, you need to use a high shutter speed.
    14 ○ 89 ○ 90

15. Zooming all the way in will minimize camera wobbles.
    15 ○ 91 ○ 92

SECTION TOTAL [ ]

PROBLEM-SOLVING APPLICATIONS

1. Locate the tilt and pan drag and lock mechanisms of the mounting head. Adjust them so that you can pan and tilt the camera as smoothly as possible.

2. Place three chairs along the z-axis about 9 feet apart. Zoom in to an ECU on the first chair. It will probably be out of focus at the end of the zoom. Now bring the picture into focus. When zooming out, the picture will remain in focus. Without touching the focus, now zoom in on the last chair. Again, the picture will probably get out of focus when reaching the ECU of the last chair. Now focus on the last chair and zoom back out. Without adjusting the focus, zoom in on the second chair, zoom back, and then zoom in again on the last chair. Will the second as well as the last chair remain in focus during the zoom-in? If so, why? If not, why not?

3. With your knees pointing in the direction of the start of the pan, pan the camera slowly and smoothly about 100 degrees. Now repeat the same pan with your knees preset as much as possible in the direction of the end point of the pan. Which position makes for a smoother pan? Why?

4. With the automatic white balance turned off, video-record for a few seconds a white object (such as a small white card) outdoors, then repeat the same shot with indoor lighting (such as with your reading lamp shining on it) and then under fluorescent lights. Compare the various color tints of the "white" card. Repeat the same procedure but with the automatic white balance turned on or by white-balancing for each of the illuminations. Now do the colors of the white object look the same in each shot? Why?

5. With a handheld or shoulder-mounted camcorder, follow a friend from behind and video-record him or her while walking along the z-axis. Now do the same while walking backward and having your friend face the camera during the video-recording. Which version made it easier for you to keep the camera steady? Why?

6. You happen to overhear one of the camera operators of a multicamera production brag about never using the locking mechanism of the mounting head when leaving the camera unattended; she says she uses a tighter pan-and-tilt adjustment instead. She says that this will add a minute to her coffee break. What is your reaction? Be specific.

6 Looking Through the Viewfinder

REVIEW OF KEY TERMS

Match each term with its appropriate definition by filling in the corresponding bubble.

1. psychological closure
2. headroom
3. noseroom
4. depth of field

5. field of view
6. z-axis
7. close-up
8. vector

9. medium shot
10. long shot
11. aspect ratio
12. over-the-shoulder shot

A. Object or any part of it seen at close range

B. A directional screen force

C. The relationship of screen width to screen height

A
( )1 ( )2 ( )3 ( )4
( )5 ( )6 ( )7 ( )8
( )9 ( )10 ( )11 ( )12

B
( )1 ( )2 ( )3 ( )4
( )5 ( )6 ( )7 ( )8
( )9 ( )10 ( )11 ( )12

C
( )1 ( )2 ( )3 ( )4
( )5 ( )6 ( )7 ( )8
( )9 ( )10 ( )11 ( )12

PAGE TOTAL [   ]

1.	psychological closure	5.	field of view	9.	medium shot
2.	headroom	6.	z-axis	10.	long shot
3.	noseroom	7.	close-up	11.	aspect ratio
4.	depth of field	8.	vector	12.	over-the-shoulder shot

D. Object seen from far away or framed very loosely

D
○ ○ ○ ○
1 2 3 4
○ ○ ○ ○
5 6 7 8
○ ○ ○ ○
9 10 11 12

E. Mentally filling in missing visual information that will lead to a complete and stable configuration

E
○ ○ ○ ○
1 2 3 4
○ ○ ○ ○
5 6 7 8
○ ○ ○ ○
9 10 11 12

F. The space left between the top of the head and the upper screen edge

F
○ ○ ○ ○
1 2 3 4
○ ○ ○ ○
5 6 7 8
○ ○ ○ ○
9 10 11 12

G. Camera looks over the camera-near person's shoulder

G
○ ○ ○ ○
1 2 3 4
○ ○ ○ ○
5 6 7 8
○ ○ ○ ○
9 10 11 12

H. Object seen from a midrange distance

H
○ ○ ○ ○
1 2 3 4
○ ○ ○ ○
5 6 7 8
○ ○ ○ ○
9 10 11 12

PAGE
TOTAL

I. The space left in front of a person looking toward the edge of the screen

I ○ ○ ○ ○
  1 2 3 4
  ○ ○ ○ ○
  5 6 7 8
  ○ ○ ○ ○
  9 10 11 12

J. The portion of a scene visible through a particular lens; its vista

J ○ ○ ○ ○
  1 2 3 4
  ○ ○ ○ ○
  5 6 7 8
  ○ ○ ○ ○
  9 10 11 12

K. The area in which all objects, located at different distances from the camera, are in focus

K ○ ○ ○ ○
  1 2 3 4
  ○ ○ ○ ○
  5 6 7 8
  ○ ○ ○ ○
  9 10 11 12

L. Indicates screen depth; extends from camera lens to horizon

L ○ ○ ○ ○
  1 2 3 4
  ○ ○ ○ ○
  5 6 7 8
  ○ ○ ○ ○
  9 10 11 12

PAGE TOTAL [ ]

SECTION TOTAL [ ]

REVIEW OF FRAMING A SHOT AND PICTURE COMPOSITION

Select the correct answers and fill in the bubbles with the corresponding numbers.

1. The aspect ratio of the HDTV screen is (13) *4 × 3* (14) *4 × 9* (15) *16 × 9*.

2. Using the following set of numbered images, fill in the corresponding bubble for each of the fields of view or other shot designations listed below.

16

17

18

19

20

21

22

23

24

    a. MS (medium shot)

    b. LS (long shot)

1 ◯ ◯ ◯
   13   14   15

2a ◯ ◯ ◯ ◯ ◯
    16   17   18   19   20
    ◯ ◯ ◯ ◯
    21   22   23   24

2b ◯ ◯ ◯ ◯ ◯
    16   17   18   19   20
    ◯ ◯ ◯ ◯
    21   22   23   24

PAGE TOTAL

c. knee shot

2c ○ ○ ○ ○ ○
   16 17 18 19 20

○ ○ ○ ○
21 22 23 24

d. bust shot

2d ○ ○ ○ ○ ○
   16 17 18 19 20

○ ○ ○ ○
21 22 23 24

e. CU (close-up)

2e ○ ○ ○ ○ ○
   16 17 18 19 20

○ ○ ○ ○
21 22 23 24

f. three-shot

2f ○ ○ ○ ○ ○
   16 17 18 19 20

○ ○ ○ ○
21 22 23 24

g. over-the-shoulder shot (O/S)

2g ○ ○ ○ ○ ○
   16 17 18 19 20

○ ○ ○ ○
21 22 23 24

h. ECU (extreme close-up)

2h ○ ○ ○ ○ ○
   16 17 18 19 20

○ ○ ○ ○
21 22 23 24

i. ELS (extreme long shot)

2i ○ ○ ○ ○ ○
   16 17 18 19 20

○ ○ ○ ○
21 22 23 24

P A G E
T O T A L

3. Evaluate the standard framing of shots in the next eight figures by filling in the bubbles with the corresponding numbers.

a. This over-the-shoulder shot is (25) *acceptable* (26) *unacceptable*.

b. This CU is (27) *acceptable* (28) *unacceptable* because it has (29) *no headroom* (30) *too much headroom* (31) *no noseroom* (32) *sufficient clues for closure in off-screen space.* **(Fill in two bubbles.)**

c. This shot is intended to emphasize the dynamic nature of big city buildings. Its framing is (33) *acceptable* (34) *unacceptable*.

PAGE
TOTAL

d. This shot makes (35) *good* (36) *poor* use of screen depth. If depth improvement is needed, you should (37) *add foreground objects* (38) *take a tighter shot of the flags.* *(Fill in two bubbles.)*

3d ◯ ◯   ◯ ◯
35 36   37 38

e. This ECU is (39) *acceptable* (40) *unacceptable* because it has (41) *no headroom* (42) *no leadroom* (43) *sufficient clues for closure in off-screen space* (44) *insufficient clues for closure in off-screen space.* *(Fill in two bubbles.)*

3e ◯   ◯
39   40
◯ ◯ ◯ ◯
41 42 43 44

f. This shot is (45) *acceptable* (46) *unacceptable* because it has (47) *too much noseroom* (48) *too little noseroom* (49) *too much headroom* (50) *too much leadroom.* *(Fill in two bubbles.)*

3f ◯   ◯
45   46
◯ ◯ ◯ ◯
47 48 49 50

P A G E
T O T A L

g. The framing of this shot is (51) *acceptable* (52) *unacceptable* because the tilted horizon (53) *makes the shot more dynamic* (54) *is inappropriate in this context.* ***(Fill in two bubbles.)***

3g ◯ ◯　◯ ◯
　　51　52　　53　54

h. The framing of this shot is (55) *acceptable* (56) *unacceptable* because the tilted horizon (57) *makes the shot more dynamic* (58) *is inappropriate in this context.* ***(Fill in two bubbles.)***

3f ◯ ◯　◯ ◯
　　55　56　　57　58

```
P A G E
T O T A L   [        ]

SECTION
TOTAL       [        ]
```

Course No. _____ Date _____ Name _____

REVIEW OF VECTORS AND PSYCHOLOGICAL CLOSURE

1. Identify the specific vectors displayed in the following three figures by filling in the bubbles with the corresponding numbers.

a. This picture shows a prominent (59) *graphic* (60) *index* (61) *motion* vector.

1a   ◯   ◯   ◯
      59   60   61

b. This picture shows prominent (62) *graphic* (63) *index* (64) *motion* vectors.

1b   ◯   ◯   ◯
      62   63   64

c. This picture shows (65) *graphic* (66) *index* (67) *motion* vectors.

1c   ◯   ◯   ◯
      65   66   67

PAGE TOTAL [   ]

2. Evaluate the following two figures by filling in the bubbles with the corresponding numbers.

a. The framing of this shot is (68) *acceptable* (69) *unacceptable* because it (70) *leads us to undesirable closure within the frame* (71) *leads us to undesirable closure in off-screen space* (72) *leads us to desirable closure in off-screen space* (73) *prevents closure.* ***(Fill in two bubbles.)***

b. The framing of this shot is (74) *acceptable* (75) *unacceptable* because it (76) *leads us to undesirable closure within the frame* (77) *leads us to undesirable closure in off-screen space* (78) *leads us to desirable closure in off-screen space* (79) *prevents closure.* ***(Fill in two bubbles.)***

2b 74 75 76 77 78 79

P A G E
T O T A L

SECTION
TOTAL

REVIEW OF LENSES, DEPTH OF FIELD, AND Z-AXIS MANIPULATION

Select the correct answers and fill in the bubbles with the corresponding numbers.

1. A wide-angle lens position gives you a relatively (80) *shallow* (81) *wide* (82) *great* depth of field.

1	○ 80	○ 81	○ 82

2. A narrow-angle lens position gives you a relatively (83) *shallow* (84) *wide* (85) *great* depth of field.

2	○ 83	○ 84	○ 85

3. The figure below shows the camera zoomed out all the way for a wide-angle view and focused on object A. Object B will probably be (86) *in focus* (87) *out of focus*. The depth of field is therefore (88) *great* (89) *shallow*. ***(Fill in two bubbles.)***

3	○ 86	○ 87	○ 88	○ 89

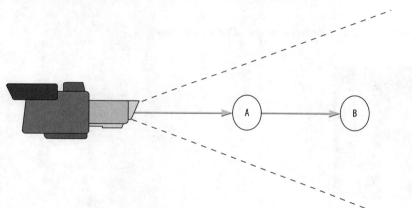

4. The figure below shows the camera zoomed in all the way for a telephoto view and focused on object A. Object B will probably be (90) *in focus* (91) *out of focus*. The depth of field is therefore (92) *great* (93) *shallow*. ***(Fill in two bubbles.)***

4	○ 90	○ 91	○ 92	○ 93

5. The area in which all objects, although located at different distances from the camera, are in focus is called (94) *depth of focus* (95) *field of view* (96) *depth of field*.

5	○ 94	○ 95	○ 96

PAGE TOTAL ☐

6. The preview monitors for cameras 1, 2, and 3 display the following images. Assuming that all three cameras are positioned right next to one another, what is the approximate zoom position for each? Choose among (97) *wide angle (short focal length)* (98) *normal (medium focal length)* and (99) *narrow angle (long focal length)*.

a—Camera 1   **b**—Camera 2   **c**—Camera 3

6a ○ 97   ○ 98   ○ 99

6b ○ 97   ○ 98   ○ 99

6c ○ 97   ○ 98   ○ 99

7. The screen image below shows that the camera's zoom lens was in a (100) *wide-angle* (101) *narrow-angle* position.

7 ○ 100   ○ 101

8. The screen image below displays a (102) *great* (103) *shallow* depth of field.

8 ○ 102   ○ 103

PAGE TOTAL

SECTION TOTAL

REVIEW QUIZ

*Mark the following statements as true or false by filling in the bubbles in the **T** (for true) or **F** (for false) column.*

		T	F
1.	In general, video is more of a close-up than a long-shot medium.	◯ 104	◯ 105
2.	Leadroom and noseroom fulfill similar framing (compositional) functions.	◯ 106	◯ 107
3.	Wide-angle zoom positions slow down perceived z-axis speed.	◯ 108	◯ 109
4.	There is no aesthetic difference between a zoom and a dolly.	◯ 110	◯ 111
5.	You should always try to achieve psychological closure within the TV screen area.	◯ 112	◯ 113
6.	Psychological closure always ensures good composition.	◯ 114	◯ 115
7.	The focal length of lenses has considerable influence on the depth of field.	◯ 116	◯ 117
8.	Close-ups normally have a shallow depth of field.	◯ 118	◯ 119
9.	An effective close-up should provide visual clues for closure in off-screen space.	◯ 120	◯ 121
10.	When following lateral motion, you should keep as little space as possible between the object and the screen edge toward which the object is moving.	◯ 122	◯ 123
11.	Z-axis blocking is especially advantageous for the small screen.	◯ 124	◯ 125
12.	The focal length of the lens has little influence on how we perceive z-axis blocking.	◯ 126	◯ 127
13.	The aperture of a lens influences the depth of field.	◯ 128	◯ 129
14.	A tilted horizon line can make the composition less stable and more dynamic.	◯ 130	◯ 131
15.	Wide vistas are easier to frame in the 16 × 9 aspect ratio than in the 4 × 3 aspect ratio.	◯ 132	◯ 133

SECTION TOTAL ☐

PROBLEM-SOLVING APPLICATIONS

1. With your camcorder in the wide-angle zoom lens position, walk toward an object. Go back to your starting point and this time zoom in on the object. When playing back the two scenes, can you tell which was the dolly and which was the zoom? How?

2. When watching television or a movie, try to figure out what lenses (zoom lens positions) were used for some of the shots. For example, when you see someone running toward the camera yet seemingly not getting closer, what lens was used? Or when you see the happy couple approach the dinner table through the out-of-focus flowers and candles in the foreground, what lens was probably used? Such observations will help you become more aware of focal lengths and their effects. Compare your notes with those of others watching the same program or movie.

3. Your documentary is to show the congestion and the lack of breathing space between the units in a new suburban housing development. When aiming your camera along the street, what zoom lens position would you use? Why?

4. The director wants the foreground object in focus but the background out of focus. How can you accomplish this request?

5. The director tells you, the camera operator, to change from a cross-shot to an over-the-shoulder shot. What does the director mean? How can you accomplish such a shot change?

6. Zoom all the way out with your camcorder and focus on an object about 4 to 6 feet away from you. Look at the background objects (about 20 feet away from you). Are they visible? Do they appear in fairly sharp focus or are they blurred? Next make the same observations by backing up a little with your camera and zooming in all the way on the camera-near object. Is the background still clearly visible? Relate your observations to depth of field.

7. When your two HDTV studio cameras focus on the interview set, you discover that some of the background flaws become clearly visible and distracting. What can you do in the last minute before the scheduled video recording?

8. When simulating a z-axis crowd, should you use a wide-angle or narrow-angle zoom lens position? Why?

Image Creation: Sound, Light, Graphics, and Effects

7 Audio and Sound Control

REVIEW OF KEY TERMS

Match each term with its appropriate definition by filling in the corresponding bubble.

1. omnidirectional
2. pickup pattern
3. hypercardioid
4. polar pattern
5. cardioid
6. unidirectional

7. ribbon microphone
8. dynamic microphone
9. windscreen
10. lavalier
11. VU meter

12. pop filter
13. XLR
14. sweetening
15. condenser microphone
16. fader

A. A professional three-wire connector for audio cables

A
1 2 3 4
5 6 7 8
9 10 11 12
13 14 15 16

B. Acoustic foam rubber that is put over the microphone to cut down wind noise in outdoor use

B
1 2 3 4
5 6 7 8
9 10 11 12
13 14 15 16

PAGE TOTAL

1. omnidirectional	7. ribbon microphone	12. pop filter
2. pickup pattern	8. dynamic microphone	13. XLR
3. hypercardioid	9. windscreen	14. sweetening
4. polar pattern	10. lavalier	15. condenser microphone
5. cardioid	11. VU meter	16. fader
6. unidirectional		

C. A narrow, highly directional pickup pattern

C
1 2 3 4
5 6 7 8
9 10 11 12
13 14 15 16

D. A small microphone that is clipped onto clothing

D
1 2 3 4
5 6 7 8
9 10 11 12
13 14 15 16

E. A heart-shaped pickup pattern

E
1 2 3 4
5 6 7 8
9 10 11 12
13 14 15 16

F. A microphone that can mainly hear sounds that come from the front

F
1 2 3 4
5 6 7 8
9 10 11 12
13 14 15 16

PAGE TOTAL

G. A microphone that can hear equally well from all directions

G 1 2 3 4 5 6 7 8 9 10 11 12 13 14 15 16

H. The two-dimensional representation of the pickup pattern

H 1 2 3 4 5 6 7 8 9 10 11 12 13 14 15 16

I. A relatively rugged microphone, good for outdoor use

I 1 2 3 4 5 6 7 8 9 10 11 12 13 14 15 16

J. High-quality, highly sensitive microphone for critical sound pickup; produces warm sound

J 1 2 3 4 5 6 7 8 9 10 11 12 13 14 15 16

K. The territory around the microphone within which the mic can hear well

K 1 2 3 4 5 6 7 8 9 10 11 12 13 14 15 16

PAGE TOTAL

© 2010 Wadsworth/Cengage

1. omnidirectional	7. ribbon microphone	12. pop filter
2. pickup pattern	8. dynamic microphone	13. XLR
3. hypercardioid	9. windscreen	14. sweetening
4. polar pattern	10. lavalier	15. condenser microphone
5. cardioid	11. VU meter	16. fader
6. unidirectional		

L. A sliding volume control

L
○ ○ ○ ○
1 2 3 4
○ ○ ○ ○
5 6 7 8
○ ○ ○ ○
9 10 11 12
○ ○ ○ ○
13 14 15 16

M. Wire-mesh screen attached to the front of a mic to reduce sudden air blasts

M
○ ○ ○ ○
1 2 3 4
○ ○ ○ ○
5 6 7 8
○ ○ ○ ○
9 10 11 12
○ ○ ○ ○
13 14 15 16

N. High-quality microphone with a battery power supply

N
○ ○ ○ ○
1 2 3 4
○ ○ ○ ○
5 6 7 8
○ ○ ○ ○
9 10 11 12
○ ○ ○ ○
13 14 15 16

O. Measures volume units, the relative loudness of amplified sound

O
○ ○ ○ ○
1 2 3 4
○ ○ ○ ○
5 6 7 8
○ ○ ○ ○
9 10 11 12
○ ○ ○ ○
13 14 15 16

P A G E
T O T A L

P.   Manipulating recorded sound in postproduction

P   ○ ○ ○ ○
   1 2 3 4
   ○ ○ ○ ○
   5 6 7 8
   ○ ○ ○ ○
   9 10 11 12
   ○ ○ ○ ○
  13 14 15 16

PAGE
TOTAL   [   ]

SECTION
TOTAL   [   ]

REVIEW OF SOUND-GENERATING ELEMENTS AND SOUND PICKUP

Select the correct answers and fill in the bubbles with the corresponding numbers.

1. Fill in the bubbles whose numbers correspond with the polar patterns in the following figure.

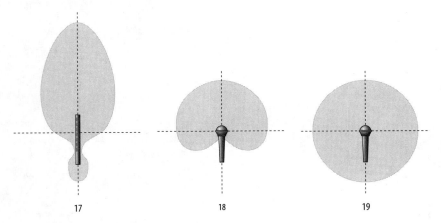

17   18   19

a. omnidirectional

b. cardioid

c. hypercardioid

2. Select the three types of microphones as classified by how they are made—their sound-generating element: (20) *cardioid* (21) *ribbon* (22) *omnidirectional* (23) *dynamic* (24) *condenser* (25) *unidirectional*. **(Fill in three bubbles.)**

3. To eliminate sudden plosive sounds when speaking close to the microphone, use a (26) *pop filter* (27) *windscreen* (28) *ribbon filter*.

4. The microphone that needs a special power supply (usually a battery) to generate the sound signal in the microphone is (29) *dynamic* (30) *ribbon* (31) *condenser*.

5. A shotgun mic has a pickup pattern that is (32) *omnidirectional* (33) *unidirectional (hypercardioid)* (34) *nondirectional*.

6. The most rugged microphones that work well outdoors are (35) *dynamic* (36) *ribbon* (37) *condenser*.

1a	○ 17	○ 18	○ 19
1b	○ 17	○ 18	○ 19
1c	○ 17	○ 18	○ 19
2	○ 20	○ 21	○ 22
	○ 23	○ 24	○ 25
3	○ 26	○ 27	○ 28
4	○ 29	○ 30	○ 31
5	○ 32	○ 33	○ 34
6	○ 35	○ 36	○ 37

SECTION TOTAL

REVIEW OF MICROPHONE USE

Select the correct answers and fill in the bubbles with the corresponding numbers.

1. The most appropriate mics for the voice pickup of a four-person studio news team (two anchors, a sportscaster, and a weathercaster) are (38) *boom mics* (39) *desk mics* (40) *lavaliers* (41) *a hand mic for the weathercaster and lavaliers for the seated talent.*

   1 ◯ ◯ ◯ ◯
   38 39 40 41

2. The high-quality hand microphone normally used by singers is a (42) *dynamic* (43) *supercardioid* (44) *condenser* microphone.

   2 ◯ ◯ ◯
   42 43 44

3. The hand microphones used in ENG normally have (45) *an omnidirectional* (46) *a bidirectional* (47) *a hyper- or supercardioid* pickup pattern.

   3 ◯ ◯ ◯
   45 46 47

4. When using a shotgun mic outdoors, you should cover it with a (48) *windscreen* (49) *styrofoam casing* (50) *windsock.* **(Multiple answers are possible.)**

   4 ◯ ◯ ◯
   48 49 50

5. Boom microphones normally have (51) *a cardioid* (52) *an omnidirectional* (53) *a hyper- or supercardioid* pickup pattern.

   5 ◯ ◯ ◯
   51 52 53

6. You are to set up microphones for a six-member panel discussion. All participants sit in a row at a long table. Normally, you would use (54) *boom* (55) *hand* (56) *desk* mics for this production.

   6 ◯ ◯ ◯
   54 55 56

7. A single news anchor usually uses a (57) *lavalier* (58) *hand* (59) *boom* mic.

   7 ◯ ◯ ◯
   57 58 59

8. When interviewing a swimmer after a race, the most flexible microphone is the (60) *boom* (61) *hand* (62) *lavalier* mic.

   8 ◯ ◯ ◯
   60 61 62

9. Of the three mics listed, the most useful mic for a singer in a band is the (63) *boom* (64) *stand* (65) *lavalier* mic.

   9 ◯ ◯ ◯
   63 64 65

10. In noisy surroundings, the field reporter must speak (66) *across* (67) *into* (68) *at a right angle to* the hand mic.

    10 ◯ ◯ ◯
    66 67 68

11. When using a pencil mic on a fishpole, you can pick up the sound (69) *only from above* (70) *only from below* (71) *from above or below* the source.

    11 ◯ ◯ ◯
    69 70 71

SECTION TOTAL ▢

REVIEW OF SOUND CONTROL

Select the correct answers and fill in the bubbles with the corresponding numbers.

1. The variety of quality controls on an audio console is (72) *greater than* (73) *the same as* (74) *less than* the quality controls on an audio mixer.

   <table><tr><td>1</td><td>○
72</td><td>○
73</td><td>○
74</td></tr></table>

2. Overloading the volume of the incoming sound signal will result in (75) *distorted sound* (76) *feedback* (77) *damage to the VU meter.*

   <table><tr><td>2</td><td>○
75</td><td>○
76</td><td>○
77</td></tr></table>

3. Normally, the test tone at the beginning of a videotape leader should be (78) *–1 VU* (79) *+1 VU* (80) *0 VU.*

   <table><tr><td>3</td><td>○
78</td><td>○
79</td><td>○
80</td></tr></table>

4. For digital recording, the test tone should be (81) *0 VU* (82) *below 0 VU* (83) *above 0 VU.*

   <table><tr><td>4</td><td>○
81</td><td>○
82</td><td>○
83</td></tr></table>

Fill in the bubble whose number corresponds with the number identifying the equipment shown in the following two figures.

5. The place that marks the beginning of the "overload" zone is (84) *–5 VU* (85) *–2 VU* (86) *0 VU.*

   <table><tr><td>5</td><td>○
84</td><td>○
85</td><td>○
86</td></tr></table>

6. The various heads in the head assembly shown in the following figure are:

a. playback head	**6a** ○ 87 ○ 88 ○ 89
b. erase head	**6b** ○ 87 ○ 88 ○ 89
c. record head	**6c** ○ 87 ○ 88 ○ 89

P A G E
T O T A L [   ]

7. When plugging a mic into a camcorder or mixer, the mic cable must be plugged into the (90) *line-level* (91) *remote* (92) *mic-level* jack.

8. The various audio connectors as shown in this figure are:

93 94 95 96

    a. phone plug

    b. mini plug

    c. RCA phono plug

    d. XLR

9. Most professional mic cables use (97) *RCA phono* (98) *mini plug* (99) *XLR* connectors.

10. When recording digital audio, the VU meter (100) *can* (101) *can occasionally* (102) *should never* spill into the overload zone.

7	○ 90	○ 91	○ 92

8a	○ 93	○ 94	○ 95	○ 96
8b	○ 93	○ 94	○ 95	○ 96
8c	○ 93	○ 94	○ 95	○ 96
8d	○ 93	○ 94	○ 95	○ 96

9	○ 97	○ 98	○ 99

10	○ 100	○ 101	○ 102

PAGE TOTAL

SECTION TOTAL

REVIEW OF SOUND RECORDING AND AESTHETICS

Select the correct answers and fill in the bubbles with the corresponding numbers.

1. In the figure below, which button would you press to return to the beginning of the track currently playing?

| 103 | 104 | 105 | 106 | 107 | 108 | 109 |

2. Indicate the sound characteristics in this waveform with the corresponding numbers.

110   111   112   110   113

   a. sharp loud sounds

   b. silences

   c. increasing volume

3. Matching audio and video energies means to (114) *adjust the strength of the audio signals to those of the video signals* (115) *use similar digital effects in video and audio* (116) *have high- and low-energy audio accompany high- and low-energy video.*

4. The figure/ground principle in audio refers to (117) *a person speaking while moving against a stable background* (118) *making the principal sound source as loud as the background sounds* (119) *separating the principal sound source from the background sounds through a higher volume.*

5. Sound perspective is especially important when the director cuts frequently from (120) *CU to CU* (121) *CU to LS and reverse* (122) *0/S to 0/S from the reverse side.*

1
○ 103 ○ 104 ○ 105 ○ 106
○ 107 ○ 108 ○ 109

2a ○ 110 ○ 111 ○ 112 ○ 113

2b ○ 110 ○ 111 ○ 112 ○ 113

2c ○ 110 ○ 111 ○ 112 ○ 113

3 ○ 114   ○ 115   ○ 116

4 ○ 117   ○ 118   ○ 119

5 ○ 120   ○ 121   ○ 122

SECTION TOTAL

REVIEW QUIZ

*Mark the following statements as true or false by filling in the bubbles in the **T** (for true) or*
***F** (for false) column.*

		T	F
1.	Regardless of whether you work with a mixer or an audio console, each input has its own pot (fader).	**1** ○ 123	○ 124
2.	Dynamic mics are generally less sensitive to shock and temperature extremes than are condenser mics.	**2** ○ 125	○ 126
3.	Riding gain means adjusting the signal so that it continuously reads *0* regardless of the input audio levels.	**3** ○ 127	○ 128
4.	To test whether a microphone is turned on, you should blow into it.	**4** ○ 129	○ 130
5.	You should always use AGC when doing a field pickup.	**5** ○ 131	○ 132
6.	Lavalier microphones are useful for news anchors.	**6** ○ 133	○ 134
7.	When riding gain, you should keep the VU needle between 60 and 100 (–5 and 0).	**7** ○ 135	○ 136
8.	Because lavalier microphones are highly sensitive, they work best when hidden under a shirt or blouse.	**8** ○ 137	○ 138
9.	Digital audio can be recorded on a solid-state (SD) device but not on videotape.	**9** ○ 139	○ 140
10.	Digital sound is less sensitive to distortion than analog sound when riding gain between 0 and +1 VU.	**10** ○ 141	○ 142
11.	Because there are adapters, you don't have to worry about the cable connectors' fitting the equipment jacks.	**11** ○ 143	○ 144
12.	A pencil mic is a good fishpole pickup method for a two-way conversation.	**12** ○ 145	○ 146
13.	Once you use an external microphone, you should turn off the camera mic.	**13** ○ 147	○ 148
14.	In EFP you should try to mix the sounds as carefully as possible with the use of a portable mixer.	**14** ○ 149	○ 150
15.	Line-level inputs are used for relatively high-level inputs.	**15** ○ 151	○ 152
16.	All microphones are insensitive to shock once they are turned off.	**16** ○ 153	○ 154

SECTION TOTAL [   ]

PROBLEM-SOLVING APPLICATIONS

1. The new PA tells you that the audio engineer of his former employer used lavalier microphones exclusively on the actors of a college play because lavs would provide excellent sound perspective without driving the audio console operator crazy. Do you agree with this audio engineer? If so, why? If not, why not?

2. While riding gain during a digital live recording of a small rock band, the director is concerned about overmodulation when the VU meters occasionally peak into the +1 red zone. What is your response?

3. You are doing a documentary on police patrols in your city. You first want to hear the conversations and the police radio inside the patrol car and then capture the sounds of possible conversations, yelling, or any other audio when the officers leave the patrol car to confront a suspect. What microphones would you need for optimal sound pickup in these situations?

4. During a short segment of an EFP in an auto assembly plant, the new PA wonders why the audio people do not try mixing the ambient sounds with the voices of the reporter and the plant supervisor right on the spot. He feels that mixing in the field would eliminate the need for a great deal of postproduction sweetening. What are your comments?

5. You are in charge of audio for a show that consists of several intimate numbers by a singer and a small band. After the rehearsal an observer in the control room tells you that the singer holds the mic during the softer passages much too close to her mouth and that she should hold the mic much lower and sing "across" rather than into it. What is your reaction? Why?

6. The EFP director blames the fishpole operator for the excessive wind noise during an outdoor interview. The fishpole operator blames the director for conducting the interview at a windy street corner and insists that even a windsock would not have prevented the wind noise distortion. What is your reaction? Be specific.

Light, Color, and Lighting

REVIEW OF KEY TERMS

Match each term with its appropriate definition by filling in the corresponding bubble.

1. directional light
2. diffused light
3. baselight
4. lux
5. foot-candle
6. attached shadow
7. cast shadow

8. falloff
9. additive primary colors
10. color temperature
11. spotlight
12. floodlight
13. contrast

14. photographic principle
15. key light
16. fill light
17. back light
18. background light
19. light plot

A. Lighting instrument that produces diffused light

B. European standard for measuring light intensity

75

1. directional light	8. falloff	14. photographic principle
2. diffused light	9. additive primary colors	15. key light
3. baselight	10. color temperature	16. fill light
4. lux	11. spotlight	17. back light
5. foot-candle	12. floodlight	18. background light
6. attached shadow	13. contrast	19. light plot
7. cast shadow		

C. Even, nondirectional light necessary for the camera to operate optimally; refers to the overall light intensity

C
○ ○ ○ ○ ○
1 2 3 4 5
○ ○ ○ ○ ○
6 7 8 9 10
○ ○ ○ ○ ○
11 12 13 14 15
○ ○ ○ ○
16 17 18 19

D. Lighting instrument that produces directional, relatively undiffused light

D
○ ○ ○ ○ ○
1 2 3 4 5
○ ○ ○ ○ ○
6 7 8 9 10
○ ○ ○ ○ ○
11 12 13 14 15
○ ○ ○ ○
16 17 18 19

E. Illumination of the set pieces and the backdrop

E
○ ○ ○ ○ ○
1 2 3 4 5
○ ○ ○ ○ ○
6 7 8 9 10
○ ○ ○ ○ ○
11 12 13 14 15
○ ○ ○ ○
16 17 18 19

PAGE TOTAL

F. Shadow that is produced by an object and thrown on another surface; it can be independent of the object

F
○ ○ ○ ○ ○
1 2 3 4 5
○ ○ ○ ○ ○
6 7 8 9 10
○ ○ ○ ○ ○
11 12 13 14 15
○ ○ ○ ○
16 17 18 19

G. The difference between the lightest and the darkest spot in a picture

G
○ ○ ○ ○ ○
1 2 3 4 5
○ ○ ○ ○ ○
6 7 8 9 10
○ ○ ○ ○ ○
11 12 13 14 15
○ ○ ○ ○
16 17 18 19

H. The speed (degree) with which a light picture portion turns into shadow areas; it can be fast or slow

H
○ ○ ○ ○ ○
1 2 3 4 5
○ ○ ○ ○ ○
6 7 8 9 10
○ ○ ○ ○ ○
11 12 13 14 15
○ ○ ○ ○
16 17 18 19

I. The standard arrangement of key, back, and fill lights, with the back light opposite the camera and directly behind the object, and the key and fill lights on opposite sides of the camera and to the front and side of the object

I
○ ○ ○ ○ ○
1 2 3 4 5
○ ○ ○ ○ ○
6 7 8 9 10
○ ○ ○ ○ ○
11 12 13 14 15
○ ○ ○ ○
16 17 18 19

P A G E
T O T A L

1. directional light	8. falloff	14. photographic principle
2. diffused light	9. additive primary colors	15. key light
3. baselight	10. color temperature	16. fill light
4. lux	11. spotlight	17. back light
5. foot-candle	12. floodlight	18. background light
6. attached shadow	13. contrast	19. light plot
7. cast shadow		

J. A plan, similar to a floor plan, that shows the type and the location of the lighting instruments relative to the scene to be illuminated and the general direction of the beams

K. Shadow that is on the object itself; it cannot be seen independent of the object

L. Illumination from behind the subject and opposite the camera

J   ○ ○ ○ ○ ○
    1   2   3   4   5
    ○ ○ ○ ○ ○
    6   7   8   9   10
    ○ ○ ○ ○ ○
    11   12   13   14   15
    ○ ○ ○ ○
    16   17   18   19

K   ○ ○ ○ ○ ○
    1   2   3   4   5
    ○ ○ ○ ○ ○
    6   7   8   9   10
    ○ ○ ○ ○ ○
    11   12   13   14   15
    ○ ○ ○ ○
    16   17   18   19

L   ○ ○ ○ ○ ○
    1   2   3   4   5
    ○ ○ ○ ○ ○
    6   7   8   9   10
    ○ ○ ○ ○ ○
    11   12   13   14   15
    ○ ○ ○ ○
    16   17   18   19

PAGE TOTAL

M. Light that causes relatively soft shadows

M	○ 1	○ 2	○ 3	○ 4	○ 5
	○ 6	○ 7	○ 8	○ 9	○ 10
	○ 11	○ 12	○ 13	○ 14	○ 15
	○ 16	○ 17	○ 18	○ 19	

N. Additional light on the opposite side of the camera from the key light to illuminate shadow areas and thereby reduce falloff

N	○ 1	○ 2	○ 3	○ 4	○ 5
	○ 6	○ 7	○ 8	○ 9	○ 10
	○ 11	○ 12	○ 13	○ 14	○ 15
	○ 16	○ 17	○ 18	○ 19	

O. The American unit for measuring light intensity

O	○ 1	○ 2	○ 3	○ 4	○ 5
	○ 6	○ 7	○ 8	○ 9	○ 10
	○ 11	○ 12	○ 13	○ 14	○ 15
	○ 16	○ 17	○ 18	○ 19	

P. Red, green, and blue

P	○ 1	○ 2	○ 3	○ 4	○ 5
	○ 6	○ 7	○ 8	○ 9	○ 10
	○ 11	○ 12	○ 13	○ 14	○ 15
	○ 16	○ 17	○ 18	○ 19	

P A G E
TOTAL

1. directional light
2. diffused light
3. baselight
4. lux
5. foot-candle
6. attached shadow
7. cast shadow
8. falloff
9. additive primary colors
10. color temperature
11. spotlight
12. floodlight
13. contrast
14. photographic principle
15. key light
16. fill light
17. back light
18. background light
19. light plot

Q. Relative reddishness or bluishness of light, as measured on the Kelvin scale

Q 1 2 3 4 5 6 7 8 9 10 11 12 13 14 15 16 17 18 19

R. Light that causes sharp shadows

R 1 2 3 4 5 6 7 8 9 10 11 12 13 14 15 16 17 18 19

S. Principal source of illumination

S 1 2 3 4 5 6 7 8 9 10 11 12 13 14 15 16 17 18 19

PAGE TOTAL

SECTION TOTAL

REVIEW OF LIGHT, SHADOWS, AND COLOR

Select the correct answers and fill in the bubbles with the corresponding numbers.

1. Electronic white balance (20) *makes a white object look white by the camera regardless of the relative color temperature of the light* (21) *controls extremely bright spots in the picture* (22) *adjusts the brightness in the viewfinder.*

   1 ○ 20   ○ 21   ○ 22

2. Baselight levels are measured in (23) *lux* (24) *foot-candles* (25) *f-stops.* **(Multiple answers are possible.)**

   2 ○ 23   ○ 24   ○ 25

3. One foot-candle is approximately (26) *5* (27) *10* (28) *15* lux.

   3 ○ 26   ○ 27   ○ 28

4. When lighting for slow falloff in large areas, you should use predominantly (29) *directional* (30) *diffused* (31) *high-color-temperature* light.

   4 ○ 29   ○ 30   ○ 31

5. Fast falloff means that there is (32) *a great difference between the light side and the attached-shadow side of the object* (33) *a great difference between the light side and the cast shadow* (34) *little difference between the light side and the attached-shadow side of the object.*

   5 ○ 32   ○ 33   ○ 34

6. When measuring reflected light, you must stand next to the lighted object and point the light meter (35) *toward the camera lens* (36) *toward the object* (37) *into the lights.*

   6 ○ 35   ○ 36   ○ 37

7. The standard color temperature for outdoor lighting is (38) *3,200K* (39) *3,600K* (40) *5,600K.*

   7 ○ 38   ○ 39   ○ 40

8. Contrast is measured by reading the (41) *brightest and darkest areas in the scene* (42) *highest and lowest color temperatures in a scene* (43) *foreground light and background light.*

   8 ○ 41   ○ 42   ○ 43

9. The standard color temperature for indoor lighting is (44) *3,200K* (45) *3,600K* (46) *5,600K.*

   9 ○ 44   ○ 45   ○ 46

10. A high color temperature means that the light has a (47) *reddish* (48) *bluish* (49) *greenish* tinge.

    10 ○ 47   ○ 48   ○ 49

11. When measuring incident light, you must stand next to the lighted object and point the light meter (50) *toward the camera lens* (51) *toward the object* (52) *toward the background.*

    11 ○ 50   ○ 51   ○ 52

12. When all three electron guns in a color monitor hit the three additive color dots at maximum intensity, the screen will be (53) *white* (54) *black* (55) *multicolored.*

    12 ○ 53   ○ 54   ○ 55

13. When lowering the color temperature, the white light becomes more (56) *reddish* (57) *greenish* (58) *bluish.*

    13 ○ 56   ○ 57   ○ 58

SECTION TOTAL [ ]

REVIEW OF LIGHTING INSTRUMENTS

1. Fill in the bubbles whose numbers correspond with the appropriate lighting instruments shown below:

59

60

61

62

63

64

65

66

67

a. Omni-light

b. scoop

c. fluorescent bank

d. softlight

e. diffusion tent

f. Fresnel spotlight

g. clip light

h. EFP floodlight (V-light)

i. ellipsoidal spotlight

1a ○ ○ ○ ○ ○
59 60 61 62 63
○ ○ ○ ○
64 65 66 67

1b ○ ○ ○ ○ ○
59 60 61 62 63
○ ○ ○ ○
64 65 66 67

1c ○ ○ ○ ○ ○
59 60 61 62 63
○ ○ ○ ○
64 65 66 67

1d ○ ○ ○ ○ ○
59 60 61 62 63
○ ○ ○ ○
64 65 66 67

1e ○ ○ ○ ○ ○
59 60 61 62 63
○ ○ ○ ○
64 65 66 67

1f ○ ○ ○ ○ ○
59 60 61 62 63
○ ○ ○ ○
64 65 66 67

1g ○ ○ ○ ○ ○
59 60 61 62 63
○ ○ ○ ○
64 65 66 67

1h ○ ○ ○ ○ ○
59 60 61 62 63
○ ○ ○ ○
64 65 66 67

1i ○ ○ ○ ○ ○
59 60 61 62 63
○ ○ ○ ○
64 65 66 67

P A G E
T O T A L

Select the correct answers and fill in the bubbles with the corresponding numbers.

2. To flood (spread) the light beam of a Fresnel spotlight, you need to move the lamp-reflector unit (68) *toward* (69) *away from* the lens; to focus the beam more narrowly, move it (70) *toward* (71) *away from* the lens. **(Fill in two bubbles.)**

3. The flooded beam has (72) *more* (73) *less* intensity than the focused beam.

4. Open-face portable spotlights have (74) *a Fresnel lens* (75) *no lens* and (76) *a reflector* (77) *no reflector*. **(Fill in two bubbles.)**

5. A scoop has (78) *a Fresnel lens* (79) *no lens* and (80) *a focus control* (81) *no focus control*. **(Fill in two bubbles.)**

2	○ 68	○ 69	○ 70	○ 71
3	○ 72	○ 73		
4	○ 74	○ 75	○ 76	○ 77
5	○ 78	○ 79	○ 80	○ 81

P A G E
T O T A L

S E C T I O N
T O T A L

REVIEW OF LIGHTING TECHNIQUES

Select the correct answers and fill in the bubbles with the corresponding numbers.

1. The arrangement of lighting instruments shown in the figure below is generally called
(82) *triangle lighting or the basic photographic principle* (83) *photographic lighting*
(84) *the field lighting principle.*

Camera

2. Fill in the bubbles whose numbers correspond with the functions of lighting
instruments shown in the figure above and whether they are usually (88) *spotlights* or
(89) *floodlights.* **(Fill in two bubbles.)**

a. key

b. back

c. fill

1 ○ 82   ○ 83   ○ 84

2a ○ 85   ○ 86   ○ 87
      ○ 88   ○ 89

2b ○ 85   ○ 86   ○ 87
      ○ 88   ○ 89

2c ○ 85   ○ 86   ○ 87
      ○ 88   ○ 89

P A G E
T O T A L [   ]

3. What major light sources were used for illuminating the on-screen person in the following three pictures? In the diagrams, circle the instrument or instruments used, then fill in the bubbles whose numbers correspond with the instruments used to light the subject. *(Multiple answers are possible.)*

a.

b.

3a ○ ○ ○ ○
    90 91 92 93

3b ○ ○ ○ ○
    94 95 96 97

P A G E
T O T A L

c.

3c ○ ○ ○ ○
98 98 100 101

d.

3d ○ ○ ○ ○
102 103 104 105

4. Having somebody stand in front of a brightly illuminated building will (106) *provide much needed back light* (107) *help separate the person from the background* (108) *cause an undesirable silhouette effect.*

4 ○ ○ ○
106 107 108

5. When shooting an ENG interview in bright sunlight, the most convenient fill light is a (109) *large spot* (110) *scoop* (111) *reflector.*

5 ○ ○ ○
109 110 111

6. When trying to match the color temperature of outdoor light coming into a room through a window with that of your standard portable floodlights, you need to (112) *lower* (113) *raise* the color temperature of your indoor lights by putting (114) *an amber (warm orange)* (115) *a light blue* gel (filter) in front of all indoor instruments. *(Fill in two bubbles.)*

6 ○ ○ ○ ○
112 113 114 115

P A G E
T O T A L ____

S E C T I O N
T O T A L ____

REVIEW QUIZ

*Mark the following statements as true or false by filling in the bubbles in the **T** (for true) or **F** (for false) column.*

		T	F
1.	Back lights and background lights fulfill similar functions.	○ 116	○ 117
2.	Portable openface lights have no lens.	○ 118	○ 119
3.	The basic photographic principle uses a key light, a fill light, and a spotlight.	○ 120	○ 121
4.	The more fill light, the slower the falloff.	○ 122	○ 123
5.	All professional floodlights have Fresnel lenses.	○ 124	○ 125
6.	Color temperature refers to how hotly a light burns.	○ 126	○ 127
7.	You can use a floodlight for a key.	○ 128	○ 129
8.	An amber or orange gel in front of a lighting instrument will raise its color temperature.	○ 130	○ 131
9.	The background light must strike the background from the same side as the key light.	○ 132	○ 133
10.	Fluorescent banks produce fast falloff.	○ 134	○ 135
11.	C-clamps are built for mounting spotlights but not floodlights.	○ 136	○ 137
12.	Barn doors are primarily used to slow down falloff.	○ 138	○ 139
13.	Floodlights are the quickest way to illuminate a large area with even light.	○ 140	○ 141
14.	We measure color temperature on the Kelvin scale.	○ 142	○ 143
15.	High-key lighting means that the key light is situated above eye level.	○ 144	○ 145
16.	The best lighting instrument for EFP is the 2,000-watt Fresnel spotlight.	○ 146	○ 147
17.	We measure incident light by pointing the light meter close to the lighted object.	○ 148	○ 149
18.	Fill lights can easily be substituted by a reflector.	○ 150	○ 151
19.	An overcast day produces low-contrast lighting.	○ 152	○ 153
20.	Softlights can focus their light beam.	○ 154	○ 155

SECTION TOTAL [ ]

PROBLEM-SOLVING APPLICATIONS

1. You are asked to do the lighting for a shampoo commercial. The director wants you to make the model's blond hair look especially brilliant and glamorous. Which of the three instruments of the lighting triangle needs special attention to achieve the desired result?

2. You have very little time to light a five-member panel discussion in the multipurpose room of the local elementary school. The board members sit side-by-side behind a long table. What lighting type would you employ? What instruments would you use? Why?

3. The director of a studio interview with a prize-winning actor suggests using a softlight as the key instead of a Fresnel spot. What is your reaction? Be specific.

4. You are asked to video-record the president of a new computer company who wants to talk to her employees from behind her desk. The vice president tells you not to worry about the large window behind the president's chair because you can use the daylight streaming through the window as interesting back light. What is your reaction? What problems, if any, do you anticipate? What solutions would you suggest?

5. The novice assistant director is very worried about video-recording the high-school graduation ceremony. He said that the overcast sky will cause fast falloff and is prone to color distortion in the shadow areas. What is your reaction? Why?

9 Graphics and Effects

REVIEW OF KEY TERMS

Match each term with its appropriate definition by filling in the corresponding bubble.

1. **ESS system**
2. **DVE**
3. **super**
4. **C.G.**

5. **key**
6. **wipe**
7. **chroma key**

8. **aspect ratio**
9. **essential area**
10. **matte key**

A. A computer dedicated to the creation of letters and numbers for titles

A ○ ○ ○ ○ ○
   1 2 3 4 5
   ○ ○ ○ ○ ○
   6 7 8 9 10

B. The section of the screen seen by the home viewer despite a badly aligned TV set

B ○ ○ ○ ○ ○
   1 2 3 4 5
   ○ ○ ○ ○ ○
   6 7 8 9 10

C. The simultaneous overlay of two pictures on the same screen

C ○ ○ ○ ○ ○
   1 2 3 4 5
   ○ ○ ○ ○ ○
   6 7 8 9 10

D. The width-to-height relationship of a video screen

D ○ ○ ○ ○ ○
   1 2 3 4 5
   ○ ○ ○ ○ ○
   6 7 8 9 10

PAGE
TOTAL _____

1. ESS system	5. key	8. aspect ratio
2. DVE	6. wipe	9. essential area
3. super	7. chroma key	10. matte key
4. C.G.		

E. A transition in which one image gradually replaces the other on the screen in various configurations

E ① ② ③ ④ ⑤
   ⑥ ⑦ ⑧ ⑨ ⑩

F. Letters of a keyed title are filled with gray or a specific color through a third video source

F ① ② ③ ④ ⑤
   ⑥ ⑦ ⑧ ⑨ ⑩

G. Video effects generated by a computer

G ① ② ③ ④ ⑤
   ⑥ ⑦ ⑧ ⑨ ⑩

H. Analog electronic visual effect in which letters are cut into a base picture, making the letters seem to be printed on top of the background scene

H ① ② ③ ④ ⑤
   ⑥ ⑦ ⑧ ⑨ ⑩

I. Special effect that uses color (usually blue or green) for the backdrop of the source (foreground picture); all blue or green areas are replaced by the base picture

I ① ② ③ ④ ⑤
   ⑥ ⑦ ⑧ ⑨ ⑩

J. Stores many still video frames in digital form for easy access

J ① ② ③ ④ ⑤
   ⑥ ⑦ ⑧ ⑨ ⑩

PAGE TOTAL

SECTION TOTAL

REVIEW OF STANDARD ELECTRONIC EFFECTS

1. Fill in the bubbles whose numbers correspond with the buttons you would have to press on the pattern selector to create the various effects (a through e) illustrated in the following figures. *(Note that some numbered buttons do not apply.)*

a.

b.

1a ◯ ◯ ◯ ◯ ◯
    11 12 13 14 15
    ◯ ◯ ◯ ◯ ◯
    16 17 18 19 20

1b ◯ ◯ ◯ ◯ ◯
    11 12 13 14 15
    ◯ ◯ ◯ ◯ ◯
    16 17 18 19 20

PAGE
TOTAL [   ]

c.

d.

e.

1c ○ ○ ○ ○ ○
    11 12 13 14 15
    ○ ○ ○ ○ ○
    16 17 18 19 20

1d ○ ○ ○ ○ ○
    11 12 13 14 15
    ○ ○ ○ ○ ○
    16 17 18 19 20

1e ○ ○ ○ ○ ○
    11 12 13 14 15
    ○ ○ ○ ○ ○
    16 17 18 19 20

PAGE
TOTAL

2. Fill in the bubbles whose numbers correspond with the appropriate electronic effects shown in the following figures.

21

22

23

24

25

a. mosaic effect

b. fly effect

c. cube effect

d. horizontal stretching

e. solarization

	21	22	23	24	25
2a	○	○	○	○	○
2b	○	○	○	○	○
2c	○	○	○	○	○
2d	○	○	○	○	○
2e	○	○	○	○	○

PAGE TOTAL ☐

SECTION TOTAL ☐

*Mark the following statements as true or false by filling in the bubbles in the **T** (for true) or **F** (for false) column.*

		T	F
1.	The entire essential area must be filled with an image to show up on the TV screen.	**1** ○ 26	○ 27
2.	Show titles should be appropriate for the style of the program.	**2** ○ 28	○ 29
3.	When chroma-keying with a blue backdrop, the person who is to be keyed must wear blue.	**3** ○ 30	○ 31
4.	In the fly mode, the image can zoom only from small to large.	**4** ○ 32	○ 33
5.	You can achieve a split-screen effect by stopping a horizontal wipe midway.	**5** ○ 34	○ 35
6.	Before the C.G. can be used for a title, you must print the title on a studio card.	**6** ○ 36	○ 37
7.	Filling keyed letters with a specific color is called a matte key.	**7** ○ 38	○ 39
8.	Horizontal and vertical stretching can be done only with a digital signal.	**8** ○ 40	○ 41
9.	In DTV you don't have to worry about the essential area.	**9** ○ 42	○ 43
10.	The titles for a normal, or luminance, key must have a strong brightness contrast with the background.	**10** ○ 44	○ 45
11.	A fly effect is possible only with DVE.	**11** ○ 46	○ 47
12.	The aspect ratio of STV is 4 × 9.	**12** ○ 48	○ 49
13.	When matching color energies, we are especially concerned about color harmony.	**13** ○ 50	○ 51
14.	In a mosaic effect, the size of the "tiles" can be manipulated.	**14** ○ 52	○ 53
15.	You can use a green backdrop for a chroma key.	**15** ○ 54	○ 55
16.	Readability becomes an issue especially when the background is quite busy.	**16** ○ 56	○ 57
17.	The aspect ratio of HDTV is 16 × 9.	**17** ○ 58	○ 59
18.	A mosaic effect can be achieved with an analog special-effects generator.	**18** ○ 60	○ 61
19.	The ESS system functions like a large slide library and superfast slide projector.	**19** ○ 62	○ 63

SECTION TOTAL ☐

PROBLEM-SOLVING APPLICATIONS

1. The AD informs the director that a dancer, who is supposed to be chroma-keyed over a video-recorded cityscape scene, is wearing a saturated blue leotard. The director is quite concerned about this news but is assured by the floor manager that she and the TD have already taken care of the problem. What was the director concerned about? How did the floor manger and the TD resolve it?

2. The preview monitor shows that the title key is barely visible against the busy background because the letters of the key are almost as dark as the background and similar in hue. What would you, the director, suggest to the C.G. operator to make the key more legible?

3. You are the director of a new international interview show. Although the three guests do not normally come to the studio personally but participate in the interview via satellite hookup, you nevertheless want each guest, when interviewed, to appear on the same screen with the interviewer. The TD tells you that this cannot be done because the switcher is not equipped with DVE equipment. What is your response?

4. Your client wants you to have his new line of automobiles rotate on a cube. How could you meet his request? What equipment would you need?

5. The producer of a documentary on the homeless asks the C.G. operator to redesign the titles because they are not befitting the style of the show. What does she mean? Give examples.

Image Control:
Switching, Recording,
and Editing

10 Switcher and Switching

REVIEW OF KEY TERMS

Match each term with its appropriate definition by filling in the corresponding bubble.

1. **program bus**
2. **mix bus**
3. **key bus**
4. **preview bus**
5. **fader bar**
6. **DSK**
7. **switching**
8. **line-out**
9. **switcher**

A. A change from one video source to another and the creation of various transitions during the production

A   ○ ○ ○ ○ ○
    1 2 3 4 5
    ○ ○ ○ ○
    6 7 8 9

B. A lever on the switcher that produces transitions and effects of different speeds

B   ○ ○ ○ ○ ○
    1 2 3 4 5
    ○ ○ ○ ○
    6 7 8 9

C. A panel with rows of buttons that allow the selection and the assembly of various video sources

C   ○ ○ ○ ○ ○
    1 2 3 4 5
    ○ ○ ○ ○
    6 7 8 9

D. Rows of buttons that permit a super

D   ○ ○ ○ ○ ○
    1 2 3 4 5
    ○ ○ ○ ○
    6 7 8 9

PAGE
TOTAL [   ]

1. program bus	4. preview bus	7. switching
2. mix bus	5. fader bar	8. line-out
3. key bus	6. DSK	9. switcher

E. Row of buttons with inputs that are directly switched to the line-out

E ○ ○ ○ ○ ○
   1 2 3 4 5
  ○ ○ ○ ○
  6 7 8 9

F. Carries the final video and audio signal to the video recorder or transmitter

F ○ ○ ○ ○ ○
   1 2 3 4 5
  ○ ○ ○ ○
  6 7 8 9

G. Row of buttons to select the video source to be inserted into the background image

G ○ ○ ○ ○ ○
   1 2 3 4 5
  ○ ○ ○ ○
  6 7 8 9

H. Row of buttons that can direct an input to the preview/preset monitor

H ○ ○ ○ ○ ○
   1 2 3 4 5
  ○ ○ ○ ○
  6 7 8 9

I. A control that allows captions to be keyed over the picture (line-out signal) as it leaves the switcher

I ○ ○ ○ ○ ○
   1 2 3 4 5
  ○ ○ ○ ○
  6 7 8 9

PAGE TOTAL [ ]

SECTION TOTAL [ ]

REVIEW OF BASIC SWITCHER OPERATION

1. Fill in the bubbles whose numbers correspond with the appropriate parts of the switcher shown in the following figure.

a. fader bar

b. preview bus

c. program bus

1a ○ ○ ○ ○
  10 11 12 13
   ○ ○ ○ ○
  14 15 16 17

1b ○ ○ ○ ○
  10 11 12 13
   ○ ○ ○ ○
  14 15 16 17

1c ○ ○ ○ ○
  10 11 12 13
   ○ ○ ○ ○
  14 15 16 17

PAGE
TOTAL [   ]

d. key bus

e. downstream keyer controls

f. wipe pattern selector

g. delegation controls (mix, wipe, key)

h. key/matte controls

1d ◯ ◯ ◯ ◯
        10 11 12 13
        ◯ ◯ ◯ ◯
        14 15 16 17

1e ◯ ◯ ◯ ◯
        10 11 12 13
        ◯ ◯ ◯ ◯
        14 15 16 17

1f ◯ ◯ ◯ ◯
        10 11 12 13
        ◯ ◯ ◯ ◯
        14 15 16 17

1g ◯ ◯ ◯ ◯
        10 11 12 13
        ◯ ◯ ◯ ◯
        14 15 16 17

1h ◯ ◯ ◯ ◯
        10 11 12 13
        ◯ ◯ ◯ ◯
        14 15 16 17

P A G E T O T A L

2. Assuming that the switcher diagrams below are portions of a real switcher, you will see that several buttons have already been pressed. Some are high tally (fully lighted); others are low tally (dimly lighted). C1 is shooting a close-up of the newscaster, and C2 is framing a three-shot of the in-studio guests. (See monitor images below.) Select the correct monitor pair you would expect to see from the switcher output by filling in the corresponding bubbles.

18

Preview   Line

19

Preview   Line

20

Preview   Line

3. Select the correct monitor pair you would expect to see from the switcher output by filling in the corresponding bubbles.

Preview	Line

21

Preview	Line

22

Preview	Line

23

Preview	Line

P A G E
T O T A L

Select the correct answers and fill in the bubbles with the corresponding numbers.

4. To select the functions of a specific bus or buses, you need to activate
the (24) *downstream keyer* (25) *wipe pattern selector* (26) *specific delegation controls.*

5. Assuming that camera 1 is on the air, you can cut to the VR by pressing the
(27) *KEY button* (28) *CUT button* (29) *VR button* on the program bus.

6. The program bus will direct the selected video source to the (30) *preview monitor*
(31) *mix bus* (32) *line-out.*

7. Assuming that you are working with a Grass Valley 100 switcher, you press the (33) *DSK
and CUT* (34) *BKGD and MIX* (35) *KEY and MIX* buttons to activate the mix function of the
preset and program buses.

8. To put the screen to black when the title was keyed with the DSK, you need to press the
(36) *BLK button on the program bus* (37) *BLK button on the key bus* (38) *BLK button in the
downstream keyer section.*

4	◯ 24	◯ 25	◯ 26
5	◯ 27	◯ 28	◯ 29
6	◯ 30	◯ 31	◯ 32
7	◯ 33	◯ 34	◯ 35
8	◯ 36	◯ 37	◯ 38

PAGE TOTAL ☐

SECTION TOTAL ☐

REVIEW QUIZ

*Mark the following statements as true or false by filling in the bubbles in the **T** (for true) or **F** (for false) column.*

		T	F
1.	The length of the dissolve depends on how fast you move the fader bar from one end of travel to the other.	**1** ○ 39	○ 40
2.	The *AUTO TRANS* button on a switcher fulfills the same function as the fader bar.	**2** ○ 41	○ 42
3.	With a downstream keyer, you can add another title to one already created by the regular key bus before punching up both on the air.	**3** ○ 43	○ 44
4.	Everything punched up on the key bus will go directly to the line-out.	**4** ○ 45	○ 46
5.	You can assign the key bus a mix function.	**5** ○ 47	○ 48
6.	The switcher has a separate button for each input.	**6** ○ 49	○ 50
7.	If so delegated, the preview bus can become one of the mix buses.	**7** ○ 51	○ 52
8.	The key is one of the more useful transitions.	**8** ○ 53	○ 54
9.	When pushing the *BLK* button on the program bus, the line-out monitor goes to black even if the credits were generated by the downstream keyer.	**9** ○ 55	○ 56
10.	You can switch a cuts-only program entirely on the program bus.	**10** ○ 57	○ 58
11.	The program bus on a switcher sends the selected source directly to the line-out.	**11** ○ 59	○ 60
12.	If so delegated, the program bus can become the key bus.	**12** ○ 61	○ 62

SECTION TOTAL

PROBLEM-SOLVING APPLICATIONS

1. The director asks you, the TD, to superimpose a long shot of a dancer over a close-up of her face. First the director wants to have the long shot as the more prominent image and then slowly shift the emphasis in the super to the close-up. How, if at all, can you accomplish such an effect?

2. The director would like to have the total scene reveal itself gradually as though we were looking through a progressively expanding rectangle. She asks you to have the small rectangle start in the center of the screen with the proper TV aspect ratio and then expand to the full-size television screen. How, if at all, could you achieve this effect?

3. The producer would like to have an old-fashioned "The End" supered over the final shot of a chroma-keyed patio setting. He asks you, the TD, whether you can meet his request. How, if at all, could you achieve this effect?

4. In the multicamera live-recorded presentation of a highly precise balletlike dance piece, the director would like to use dissolves of exactly the same speed for all transitions. Can you do this? If so, how?

5. The same director would like to have several extremely quick cutting sequences during the argument scene between the prosecution and defense attorneys. She plans to cover the argument in tight cross-shots. How would you set up the switcher for these sequences?

6. Use your switcher and note which architecture elements of your switcher are similar to the Grass Valley 100 as pictured in this workbook and which are not.

7. Practice setting up special effects, storing and recalling them.

11 Video Recording

REVIEW OF KEY TERMS

Match each term with its appropriate definition by filling in the corresponding bubble.

1. audio track
2. video track
3. field log
4. Y/C component video
5. composite video
6. multimedia

7. tapeless systems
8. interactive video
9. nonlinear recording media
10. TBC
11. luminance
12. control track

13. Y/color difference component video
14. NTSC
15. flash memory device
16. video server

A. Stands for *National Television System Committee;* designates the composite signal system

A

1	2	3	4
5	6	7	8
9	10	11	12
13	14	15	16

B. A record of each take during the video-recording

B

1	2	3	4
5	6	7	8
9	10	11	12
13	14	15	16

P A G E
T O T A L

1. audio track	7. tapeless systems	13. Y/color difference component video
2. video track	8. interactive video	14. NTSC
3. field log	9. nonlinear recording media	15. flash memory device
4. Y/C component video	10. TBC	16. video server
5. composite video	11. luminance	
6. multimedia	12. control track	

C. A solid-state read/write digital storage media of limited capacity

C ○ ○ ○ ○
   1 2 3 4
   ○ ○ ○ ○
   5 6 7 8
   ○ ○ ○ ○
   9 10 11 12
   ○ ○ ○ ○
   13 14 15 16

D. A device that makes videotape edits and playback more stable

D ○ ○ ○ ○
   1 2 3 4
   ○ ○ ○ ○
   5 6 7 8
   ○ ○ ○ ○
   9 10 11 12
   ○ ○ ○ ○
   13 14 15 16

E. The area of the videotape used for recording the video information

E ○ ○ ○ ○
   1 2 3 4
   ○ ○ ○ ○
   5 6 7 8
   ○ ○ ○ ○
   9 10 11 12
   ○ ○ ○ ○
   13 14 15 16

F. A computer-driven video program that gives the viewer some control over what to see and how to see it; often used as a training device

F ○ ○ ○ ○
   1 2 3 4
   ○ ○ ○ ○
   5 6 7 8
   ○ ○ ○ ○
   9 10 11 12
   ○ ○ ○ ○
   13 14 15 16

PAGE
TOTAL

G. A system that separates the Y and C signals and treats the luminance and color as separate signals but combines them during the recording

G
○ ○ ○ ○
1 2 3 4
○ ○ ○ ○
5 6 7 8
○ ○ ○ ○
9 10 11 12
○ ○ ○ ○
13 14 15 16

H. Allow the recording, storage, and playback of audio and video information via digital storage devices other than videotape

H
○ ○ ○ ○
1 2 3 4
○ ○ ○ ○
5 6 7 8
○ ○ ○ ○
9 10 11 12
○ ○ ○ ○
13 14 15 16

I. The track that contains the sync pulses

I
○ ○ ○ ○
1 2 3 4
○ ○ ○ ○
5 6 7 8
○ ○ ○ ○
9 10 11 12
○ ○ ○ ○
13 14 15 16

J. The simultaneous computer display of text, still and moving images, and sound; usually recorded on an optical disc

J
○ ○ ○ ○
1 2 3 4
○ ○ ○ ○
5 6 7 8
○ ○ ○ ○
9 10 11 12
○ ○ ○ ○
13 14 15 16

K. Storage of video and audio material in digital form on a hard drive or read/write optical disc; each frame can be accessed by the computer independent of all others

K
○ ○ ○ ○
1 2 3 4
○ ○ ○ ○
5 6 7 8
○ ○ ○ ○
9 10 11 12
○ ○ ○ ○
13 14 15 16

PAGE TOTAL [ ]

1.	audio track	7.	tapeless systems	13.	Y/color difference component video	
2.	video track	8.	interactive video	14.	NTSC	
3.	field log	9.	nonlinear recording media	15.	flash memory device	
4.	Y/C component video	10.	TBC	16.	video server	
5.	composite video	11.	luminance			
6.	multimedia	12.	control track			

L. A system that combines the Y (black-and-white) and C (red, green, and blue) video information into a single signal

L
○ ○ ○ ○
1 2 3 4
○ ○ ○ ○
5 6 7 8
○ ○ ○ ○
9 10 11 12
○ ○ ○ ○
13 14 15 16

M. The area of the videotape used for recording the audio information

M
○ ○ ○ ○
1 2 3 4
○ ○ ○ ○
5 6 7 8
○ ○ ○ ○
9 10 11 12
○ ○ ○ ○
13 14 15 16

N. A system that keeps the Y and two manipulated C signals separate throughout the video-recording process

N
○ ○ ○ ○
1 2 3 4
○ ○ ○ ○
5 6 7 8
○ ○ ○ ○
9 10 11 12
○ ○ ○ ○
13 14 15 16

O. A high-capacity hard drive system for storage and playback of video programs

O
○ ○ ○ ○
1 2 3 4
○ ○ ○ ○
5 6 7 8
○ ○ ○ ○
9 10 11 12
○ ○ ○ ○
13 14 15 16

PAGE TOTAL

P. The brightness information of a video signal

P   ○ ○ ○ ○
     1 2 3 4

     ○ ○ ○ ○
     5 6 7 8

     ○ ○ ○ ○
     9 10 11 12

     ○ ○ ○ ○
     13 14 15 16

P A G E
T O T A L

SECTION
TOTAL

REVIEW OF VIDEOTAPE RECORDING SYSTEMS

Select the correct answers and fill in the bubbles with the corresponding numbers.

1. A single digital frame is made up of (17) *four fields* (18) *10 or more tracks* (19) *four analog frames.*

    1 ○ 17 ○ 18 ○ 19

2. A flash memory device has (20) *an optical disc drive* (21) *a hard disk drive* (22) *no moving parts.*

    2 ○ 20 ○ 21 ○ 22

3. The Y/C system is (23) *composite* (24) *component* during transport.

    3 ○ 23 ○ 24

4. To keep the quality loss to a minimum during extensive postproduction editing, you should use (25) *analog* (26) *digital* VTRs and a (27) *composite* (28) *component* system. **(Fill in two bubbles.)**

    4 ○ 25 ○ 26 ○ 27 ○ 28

5. The Y/color difference signal is (29) *composite* (30) *component.*

    5 ○ 29 ○ 30

6. Videotape can record (31) *digital information only* (32) *analog information only* (33) *both digital and analog information.*

    6 ○ 31 ○ 32 ○ 33

7. The Y/C color difference is primarily used to (34) *preserve image quality* (35) *emphasize the difference between black-and-white and color* (36) *show the differences in hue.*

    7 ○ 34 ○ 35 ○ 36

8. The Y signal is normally color coded as (37) *yellow* (38) *blue* (39) *green.*

    8 ○ 37 ○ 38 ○ 39

SECTION TOTAL [   ]

REVIEW OF THE VIDEO-RECORDING PROCESS

Select the correct answers and fill in the bubbles with the corresponding numbers.

1. Identify lines in the field log below that contain obvious errors in the time code, evaluation (OK or no good), or recording order. *(Multiple answers are possible.)*

PRODUCTION TITLE: History Series: Gold Rush PRODUCER/DIRECTOR: Elan Frank

RECORDING DATE: 07/15   LOCATION: Virginia City, Nevada

	MEDIA NUMBER	SCENE	TAKE	OK or NO GOOD	TIME CODE IN	TIME CODE OUT	EVENT / REMARKS
40	P2-1	3	2	OK	01:51:25	02:09:11	Stuart Z-axis boardwalk
41			1	OK	02:27:01	02:37:19	CU Stuart
42			3	OK	04:59:29	05:17:16	Street: Stage coach Jet plane AUDIO problem
43			4	NG	05:35:20	06:17:17	Bill FOCUS problem Z-axis boardwalk -
44			5	OK	06:30:12	06:28:26	Bill Z-axis boardwalk
45			6	OK	07:29:03	07:39:13	Bill CU
46	P2-2	6	1	NG	07:59:18	08:30:59	Ext: Saloon Horse in shot -
47			2	OK	08:38:28	09:15:12	Ext: Saloon

a. time code error

b. evaluation (OK/NG) error

c. recording order error

1a ◯ ◯ ◯ ◯
    40 41 42 43
    ◯ ◯ ◯ ◯
    44 45 46 47

1b ◯ ◯ ◯ ◯
    40 41 42 43
    ◯ ◯ ◯ ◯
    44 45 46 47

1c ◯ ◯ ◯ ◯
    40 41 42 43
    ◯ ◯ ◯ ◯
    44 45 46 47

PAGE TOTAL ☐

2. The most common video connectors are (48) *XLR* (49) *mini plug* (50) *BNC* (51) *RCA phono.* **(Multiple answers are possible.)**

3. Color bars are useful only when they are (52) *generated by the equipment you are actually using* (53) *dubbed from a color bar master tape* (54) *digitally generated.*

4. Mark the items that are part of a normal video leader: (55) *color bars* (56) *identification slate* (57) *control track display* (58) *test tone* (59) *edit decision list* (60) *video test pattern.* **(Multiple answers are possible.)**

5. To record on a videocassette, the protection tab must be in the (61) *open* (62) *closed* position, or (63) *broken off* (64) *unbroken.* **(Fill in two bubbles.)**

2	○ 48	○ 49	○ 50	○ 51

3	○ 52	○ 53	○ 54

4	○ 55	○ 56	○ 57
	○ 58	○ 59	○ 60

5	○ 61	○ 62	○ 63	○ 64

PAGE TOTAL

SECTION TOTAL

REVIEW OF NONLINEAR STORAGE SYSTEMS

Select the correct answers and fill in the bubbles with the corresponding numbers.

1. Indicate which of the following video storage devices is linear: (65) *DVD* (66) *hard drive* (67) *videotape* (68) *video server.*

2. Of the following, the "read-only" digital storage device is a (69) *flash drive* (70) *hard drive* (71) *digital VTR* (72) *standard CD-ROM.*

3. The ESS system can grab and digitize a video frame (73) *only from a digital videotape* (74) *only from an analog videotape* (75) *from any video source.*

4. The optical storage device that you can erase and reuse for a new recording of video and audio information is a (76) *CD-R* (77) *DVD* (78) *DVD-RW.*

5. Digital videotape recordings are (79) *linear* (80) *nonlinear* and (81) *allow* (82) *do not allow* random access. ***(Fill in two bubbles.)***

6. The recording system that has no moving parts is (83) *a flash memory card* (84) *an optical disc* (85) *a hard drive.*

1	◯ 65	◯ 66	◯ 67	◯ 68
2	◯ 69	◯ 70	◯ 71	◯ 72
3	◯ 73		◯ 74	◯ 75
4	◯ 76		◯ 77	◯ 78
5	◯ 79 ◯ 80		◯ 81	◯ 82
6	◯ 83		◯ 84	◯ 85

SECTION TOTAL ☐

Mark the following statements as true or false by filling in the bubbles in the **T** (for true) or **F** (for false) column.

		T	F
1.	The operational controls on a digital VTR are more complex than those of an analog VTR.	1 ○ 86	○ 87
2.	Color bars help in adjusting the colors on the playback monitor.	2 ○ 88	○ 89
3.	*NTSC signal* and *composite signal* mean the same thing.	3 ○ 90	○ 91
4.	The Y/C component system means that the color yellow has been added to the color signals.	4 ○ 92	○ 93
5.	The video leader must include a 0 VU test tone.	5 ○ 94	○ 95
6.	A TBC helps eliminate picture jitter.	6 ○ 96	○ 97
7.	You can play back a DVCAM videotape on an S-VHS recorder.	7 ○ 98	○ 99
8.	Y, R–Y, B–Y is a component video signal.	8 ○ 100	○ 101
9.	In a Y/color difference component system, the primary color signals are kept separate throughout the recording process.	9 ○ 102	○ 103
10.	All digital videotapes are linear storage devices.	10 ○ 104	○ 105
11.	A video leader should always be dubbed over from a master recording of standard video leaders.	11 ○ 106	○ 107
12.	Y/C component video and S-video are the same.	12 ○ 108	○ 109
13.	Contrary to a VR log, a field log does not need time code numbers.	13 ○ 110	○ 111
14.	Dubbing analog videotape produces much more deterioration from one generation to the next than when dubbing digital videotape.	14 ○ 112	○ 113
15.	A flash drive has no moving parts.	15 ○ 114	○ 115
16.	To record on a cassette, the tab must be intact or in the closed position.	16 ○ 116	○ 117

SECTION TOTAL ☐

PROBLEM-SOLVING APPLICATIONS

1. Your assistant shows you the first draft of an entry form for a statewide video competition. The specifications for tape formats read as follows: "Only digital recording formats will be accepted." Will you recommend any changes to this form? If so, why? If not, why not?

2. The CEO of a video production company asks you whether a Blu-ray disc can be played back on an HD DVD machine. What is your reply?

3. You are asked by the new dean of the College of Communications whether to invest in digital camcorders that use videotape as the recording media or camcorders with tapeless recording systems. Which type of system would you recommend? Why?

4. The same dean asks you about the difference between mini-cassettes and larger digital tape cassettes. What would you tell him?

5. The novice director tells you that you don't have to keep a field log because you will have to log the tapes anyway before editing. What is your reaction?

12 Postproduction: Linear and Nonlinear Editing

REVIEW OF KEY TERMS

Match each term with its appropriate definition by filling in the corresponding bubble.

1. linear editing system
2. edit controller
3. NLE system
4. SMPTE time code
5. pulse-count system

6. off-line editing
7. window dub
8. on-line editing
9. EDL
10. assemble editing

11. insert editing
12. capture
13. VR log
14. rough-cut

A. A popular address code that marks each video frame with a specific number

A
○ ○ ○ ○ ○
1 2 3 4 5
○ ○ ○ ○ ○
6 7 8 9 10
○ ○ ○ ○
11 12 13 14

B. Uses videotape as the recording medium

B
○ ○ ○ ○ ○
1 2 3 4 5
○ ○ ○ ○ ○
6 7 8 9 10
○ ○ ○ ○
11 12 13 14

C. The transfer of a camcorder video to the hard drive of a computer

C
○ ○ ○ ○ ○
1 2 3 4 5
○ ○ ○ ○ ○
6 7 8 9 10
○ ○ ○ ○
11 12 13 14

PAGE TOTAL [   ]

1. linear editing system	6. off-line editing	11. insert editing
2. edit controller	7. window dub	12. capture
3. NLE system	8. on-line editing	13. VR log
4. SMPTE time code	9. EDL	14. rough-cut
5. pulse-count system	10. assemble editing	

D. A device that facilitates various editing functions, such as marking edit-in and edit-out points

D   ① ② ③ ④ ⑤   1 2 3 4 5
    ⑥ ⑦ ⑧ ⑨ ⑩   6 7 8 9 10
    ⑪ ⑫ ⑬ ⑭   11 12 13 14

E. The capture of shots in low resolution or an editing process that is not intended for producing an edit master

E   1 2 3 4 5   6 7 8 9 10   11 12 13 14

F. Produces the final high-quality edit master tape in linear editing and recaptures selected shots in high-resolution in nonlinear editing

F   1 2 3 4 5   6 7 8 9 10   11 12 13 14

G. Another name for a preliminary off-line edit

G   1 2 3 4 5   6 7 8 9 10   11 12 13 14

H. Consists of edit-in and edit-out cues, expressed in time code numbers, and the nature of transitions between shots

H   1 2 3 4 5   6 7 8 9 10   11 12 13 14

PAGE TOTAL

I. The list of all takes and their in- and out-points used for editing; may have vector notations

I	① ② ③ ④ ⑤
	1 2 3 4 5
	⑥ ⑦ ⑧ ⑨ ⑩
	6 7 8 9 10
	⑪ ⑫ ⑬ ⑭
	11 12 13 14

J. An address code that uses the control track pulses to count elapsed time and frame numbers

J	① ② ③ ④ ⑤
	1 2 3 4 5
	⑥ ⑦ ⑧ ⑨ ⑩
	6 7 8 9 10
	⑪ ⑫ ⑬ ⑭
	11 12 13 14

K. A copy of the source tapes to a lower-quality tape format with the address code keyed into each frame

K	① ② ③ ④ ⑤
	1 2 3 4 5
	⑥ ⑦ ⑧ ⑨ ⑩
	6 7 8 9 10
	⑪ ⑫ ⑬ ⑭
	11 12 13 14

L. Adding shots on the edit master tape without the prior recording of a control track

L	① ② ③ ④ ⑤
	1 2 3 4 5
	⑥ ⑦ ⑧ ⑨ ⑩
	6 7 8 9 10
	⑪ ⑫ ⑬ ⑭
	11 12 13 14

M. Editing system that allows random access of shots

M	① ② ③ ④ ⑤
	1 2 3 4 5
	⑥ ⑦ ⑧ ⑨ ⑩
	6 7 8 9 10
	⑪ ⑫ ⑬ ⑭
	11 12 13 14

N. Produces highly stable edits; requires the prior laying of a control track on the edit master tape

N	① ② ③ ④ ⑤
	1 2 3 4 5
	⑥ ⑦ ⑧ ⑨ ⑩
	6 7 8 9 10
	⑪ ⑫ ⑬ ⑭
	11 12 13 14

PAGE TOTAL

SECTION TOTAL

REVIEW OF POSTPRODUCTION EDITING

Select the correct answers and fill in the bubbles with the corresponding numbers.

1. The preparing of a VR log is important for (15) *analog editing only* (16) *digital editing only* (17) *both digial and analog editing.*

    1 ○ 15   ○ 16   ○ 17

2. When doing assemble editing, you (18) *must prelay the control track on the edit master tape before editing* (19) *stripe all source tapes with a control track* (20) *simply copy the selected shots onto the edit master tape.*

    2 ○ 18   ○ 19   ○ 20

3. When editing video and audio separately with a linear system, you need to use (21) *assemble* (22) *audio* (23) *insert* editing.

    3 ○ 21   ○ 22   ○ 23

4. Contrary to linear systems, nonlinear systems allow (24) *random* (25) *nonrandom* (26) *sequential* access to each frame.

    4 ○ 24   ○ 25   ○ 26

5. The pulse-count editing system is (27) *more accurate* (28) *less accurate* in locating a specific frame than the time code system because it (29) *marks* (30) *does not mark* each individual frame with a specific address. *(Fill in two bubbles.)*

    5 ○ 27 ○ 28   ○ 29 ○ 30

6. When using a normal linear single-source editing system, you can perform (31) *cuts and dissolves* (32) *cuts and wipes* (33) *wipes only* (34) *cuts only.*

    6 ○ 31 ○ 32 ○ 33 ○ 34

7. Because when insert editing the record VTR (35) *will* (36) *will not* transfer the control track of the source tape, you (37) *need* (38) *do not need* to prerecord a continuous control track on the edit master tape. *(Fill in two bubbles.)*

    7 ○ 35 ○ 36   ○ 37 ○ 38

8. Linear systems (39) *allow* (40) *do not allow* random access to the source material and use (41) *videotape* (42) *computer disks* for their source media. *(Fill in two bubbles.)*

    8 ○ 39 ○ 40   ○ 41 ○ 42

9. Time code is useful for (43) *analog editing only* (44) *digital editing only* (45) *both analog and digital editing.*

    9 ○ 43   ○ 44   ○ 45

10. Fill in the bubbles whose numbers correspond with the numbers identifying the EDL mistakes in the following figure:

    8 ○ 46   ○ 47   ○ 48
       ○ 49   ○ 50   ○ 51

IN	OUT	
01 : 17 : 28 : 29	01 : 17 : 28 : 45	46
01 : 17 : 30 : 15	01 : 17 : 45 : 01	47
01 : 19 : 15 : 29	01 : 19 : 14 : 07	48
01 : 21 : 65 : 33	01 : 32 : 59 : 29	49
02 : 17 : 28 : 15	02 : 18 : 37 : 06	50
02 : 17 : 29 : 16	01 : 18 : 45 : 29	51

SECTION TOTAL

REVIEW QUIZ

*Mark the following statements as true or false by filling in the bubbles in the **T** (for true) or
F (for false) column.*

		T	F
1.	The basic principle of nonlinear editing is file management rather than tape copying.	**1** ○ 52	○ 53
2.	The expanded linear editing system needs at least two source VTRs.	**2** ○ 54	○ 55
3.	The pulse-count system marks each frame with a unique address.	**3** ○ 56	○ 57
4.	Time code must be recorded with the actual production to achieve a continuous frame address.	**4** ○ 58	○ 59
5.	On a linear system, you must use insert editing to split audio and video.	**5** ○ 60	○ 61
6.	Once the source tapes are captured, nonlinear editing systems do not use source VTRs.	**6** ○ 62	○ 63
7.	NLE systems allow random access to pictures and sound.	**7** ○ 64	○ 65
8.	An EDL is necessary only if you do nonlinear editing.	**8** ○ 66	○ 67
9.	The SMPTE time code marks each frame with a unique address.	**9** ○ 68	○ 69
10.	A window dub keys a unique time code address over each frame.	**10** ○ 70	○ 71
11.	Ordinarily, off-line editing does not produce the final edit master tape.	**11** ○ 72	○ 73
12.	All analog source tapes must be digitized before audio and video information can be stored on the NLE hard drive.	**12** ○ 74	○ 75
13.	Nonlinear systems do not need a time code.	**13** ○ 76	○ 77
14.	The edit controller for a linear editing system facilitates random access of various shots.	**14** ○ 78	○ 79
15.	You don't need two source VTRs to create a dissolve with an NLE system.	**15** ○ 80	○ 81
16.	You should use insert editing only when replacing a shot in an edit master tape.	**16** ○ 82	○ 83
17.	In nonlinear editing, the source tape video as well as the audio must be stored on a computer storage device.	**17** ○ 84	○ 85

SECTION
TOTAL [   ]

PROBLEM-SOLVING APPLICATIONS

1. You are told to skip the off-line editing step because the nonlinear editing system will produce a high-quality edit master anyway. What is your comment?

2. The director is not concerned about continuity or cutaways during the shooting phase because the nonlinear editing system makes it easy to fix continuity problems. What is your reaction? Be specific.

3. You are told that you can skip making a window dub when using an NLE system because each frame will show a time code readout on the computer screen anyhow. What is your reaction?

4. The editor of the daily *Noon News* show tells you not to bother with switching to the audio waveform because she always edits sound by what she hears rather than by looking at the waveform. Her complaint is that the audio waveforms "muddle the time line." What is your reaction? Be specific.

5. The same editor questions your need for high-end editing software (such as Final Cut Studio) and says that less complex programs, such as iMovie, are perfectly adequate if all you do is a cuts-only assembly of parts of the daily company news show. What is your reaction?

13 Editing Principles

REVIEW OF KEY TERMS

Match each term with its appropriate definition by filling in the corresponding bubble.

1. **continuity editing**
2. **complexity editing**
3. **continuing vectors**
4. **mental map**

5. **diverging vectors**
6. **jump cut**
7. **converging vectors**

8. **vector line**
9. **jogging**
10. **cutaway**

A. An imaginary line created by extending converging index vectors, or the direction of a motion vector

A ○ ○ ○ ○ ○
   1 2 3 4 5
   ○ ○ ○ ○ ○
   6 7 8 9 10

B. A shot that is used to intercut between two shots to improve continuity

B ○ ○ ○ ○ ○
   1 2 3 4 5
   ○ ○ ○ ○ ○
   6 7 8 9 10

C. Graphic vectors that extend each other, or index and motion vectors pointing and moving in the same direction

C ○ ○ ○ ○ ○
   1 2 3 4 5
   ○ ○ ○ ○ ○
   6 7 8 9 10

D. Index and motion vectors that point toward each other

D ○ ○ ○ ○ ○
   1 2 3 4 5
   ○ ○ ○ ○ ○
   6 7 8 9 10

PAGE TOTAL [   ]

1. continuity editing	5. diverging vectors	8. vector line
2. complexity editing	6. jump cut	9. jogging
3. continuing vectors	7. converging vectors	10. cutaway
4. mental map		

E. Tells us where things are or are supposed to be on- and off-screen

E ① ② ③ ④ ⑤
  1 2 3 4 5
  ⑥ ⑦ ⑧ ⑨ ⑩
  6 7 8 9 10

F. The building of an intensified screen event from carefully selected and juxtaposed shots

F ① ② ③ ④ ⑤
  1 2 3 4 5
  ⑥ ⑦ ⑧ ⑨ ⑩
  6 7 8 9 10

G. Index and motion vectors that point away from each other

G ① ② ③ ④ ⑤
  1 2 3 4 5
  ⑥ ⑦ ⑧ ⑨ ⑩
  6 7 8 9 10

H. The assembly of shots to ensure a seamless shot sequence

H ① ② ③ ④ ⑤
  1 2 3 4 5
  ⑥ ⑦ ⑧ ⑨ ⑩
  6 7 8 9 10

I. Frame-by-frame advancement of videotape, resulting in jerky motion

I ① ② ③ ④ ⑤
  1 2 3 4 5
  ⑥ ⑦ ⑧ ⑨ ⑩
  6 7 8 9 10

J. An image that jerks slightly from one screen position to another in two consecutive shots

J ① ② ③ ④ ⑤
  1 2 3 4 5
  ⑥ ⑦ ⑧ ⑨ ⑩
  6 7 8 9 10

PAGE TOTAL

SECTION TOTAL

REVIEW OF AESTHETIC PRINCIPLES OF CONTINUITY EDITING

Select the correct answers and fill in the bubbles with the corresponding numbers.

1. To preserve graphic vector continuity, observing the vector line is (11) *essential* (12) *recommended* (13) *irrelevant.*

   1 ○ 11 ○ 12 ○ 13

2. To preserve motion vector continuity, you (14) *must cross the vector line* (15) *should not cross the vector line* (16) *should ignore the vector line.*

   2 ○ 14 ○ 15 ○ 16

3. To preserve index vector continuity, you (17) *must cross the vector line* (18) *should not cross the vector line* (19) *should ignore the vector line.*

   3 ○ 17 ○ 18 ○ 19

4. The mental map includes (20) *only on-screen positions and directions* (21) *only off-screen positions and directions* (22) *both on- and off-screen positions and directions.*

   4 ○ 20 ○ 21 ○ 22

5. Vectors indicate (23) *a direction* (24) *an edit command* (25) *a specific address code.*

   5 ○ 23 ○ 24 ○ 25

6. A jump cut means that the subject is (26) *jumping up and down* (27) *causing the shots to break up at the edit point* (28) *perceived as abruptly changing from one screen position to the next.*

   6 ○ 26 ○ 27 ○ 28

7. In continuity editing you are primarily concerned with maintaining (29) *story continuity* (30) *schedule efficiency* (31) *vector continuity.*

   7 ○ 29 ○ 30 ○ 31

8. In the following figures, select the camera that is in the *wrong* place for continuity editing and fill in the corresponding bubble. Draw the principal vector line on all the figures (**a** through **d**).

32

 A

 B

 33   34

   a. over-the-shoulder shots of person A and person B

   8a ○ 32 ○ 33 ○ 34

PAGE TOTAL [   ]

b. cutting from long shots to close-ups during car race

c. cutting from speaker to audience

d. cutting from camera 1 (41) to different points of view of the bride and groom during a wedding

8b ◯ 35 ◯ 36 ◯ 37

8c ◯ 38 ◯ 39 ◯ 40

8d ◯ 41 ◯ 42 ◯ 43

P A G E
T O T A L

9. For each of the following storyboard pairs, indicate whether the shots (44) *can* (45) *cannot* be edited together to form converging index vectors.

a.

9a ◯ 44   ◯ 45

b.

9b ◯ 44   ◯ 45

c.

9c ◯ 44   ◯ 45

d.

9d ◯ 44   ◯ 45

PAGE TOTAL

10. Cutting together the two shots shown below will result in (46) *a jump cut* (47) *diverging vectors* (48) *reversal of screen direction.*

■ REVIEW QUIZ

*Mark the following statements as true or false by filling in the bubbles in the **T** (for true) or*
__F__ (for false) column.

		T	F
1.	In complexity editing, a jump cut can be used to intensify the event.	**1** ○ 49	○ 50
2.	The vector line is especially relevant for preserving screen positions and index and motion vector continuity.	**2** ○ 51	○ 52
3.	The primary function of complexity editing is to maintain the viewer's mental map.	**3** ○ 53	○ 54
4.	The mental map includes on-screen as well as off-screen positions.	**4** ○ 55	○ 56
5.	Z-axis index vectors can be converging or diverging, depending on context.	**5** ○ 57	○ 58
6.	Motion vectors cannot converge in a single shot.	**6** ○ 59	○ 60
7.	Motion vectors can be continuing or converging but not diverging.	**7** ○ 61	○ 62
8.	Postproduction editing is done primarily to fix production mistakes.	**8** ○ 63	○ 64
9.	When crossing the vector line during over-the-shoulder shooting, the talent will switch screen positions.	**9** ○ 65	○ 66
10.	Complexity editing requires a much stricter observance of the vector line principle than does continuity editing.	**10** ○ 67	○ 68

SECTION
TOTAL

PROBLEM-SOLVING APPLICATIONS

1. The new production intern suggests that you cover the New Year's parade by placing cameras exactly opposite each other on both sides of the street. How would you respond to the intern?

2. The host mispronounces the name of the guest during the video-recording of an interview. The director opts for going on rather than doing the opening again because "we can fix it in post." Do you agree with the director's decision? If so, why? If not, why not?

3. The director of a cable company production group tells you not to worry about what happens in off-screen space when editing because the "viewer" will not see what is going on in off-screen space anyway. What is your response?

4. A retired, highly experienced film director tells you to avoid jump cuts at all costs. What is your reaction?

5. When you want to cross the vector line with the camera to intensify a scene, the producer tells you that this is an absolute no-no. How would you justify "crossing the line"?

6. When watching a panel discussion, you notice that the index vectors of the host and the guests all point in the same screen-left direction. The director tells you that the viewers will know who's who, regardless of where the vectors point. What is your reaction? Be specific.

7. The producer tells you that shots that show the talent looking directly into the camera are always good because they will preserve shot continuity regardless of whether the following shots show the talent looking screen-left or screen-right. Do you agree with the producer? If so, why? If not, why not?

8. The EFP camera operator tells you not to worry about recording any cutaways because he has plenty of shots in his ESS file that can be used as cutaways. What is your reaction?

PART

V

Production Environment: Studio, Field, Postproduction, and Synthetic

14 Production Environment: Studio

◼ REVIEW OF KEY TERMS

Match each term with its appropriate definition by filling in the corresponding bubble.

1. cyclorama
2. P.L.
3. S.A.
4. intercom

5. studio control room
6. monitor
7. master control
8. flat

9. props
10. floor plan
11. I.F.B.

A. Piece of standing scenery used as background or to simulate the wall of a room

A ① ② ③ ④
    1 2 3 4
⑤ ⑥ ⑦ ⑧
    5 6 7 8
⑨ ⑩ ⑪
    9 10 11

B. A public-address loudspeaker system from the control room to the studio

B ① ② ③ ④
    1 2 3 4
⑤ ⑥ ⑦ ⑧
    5 6 7 8
⑨ ⑩ ⑪
    9 10 11

C. A diagram of scenery, properties, and set dressings drawn on a grid

C ① ② ③ ④
    1 2 3 4
⑤ ⑥ ⑦ ⑧
    5 6 7 8
⑨ ⑩ ⑪
    9 10 11

PAGE TOTAL ▢

1.	cyclorama	5.	studio control room	9.	props
2.	P.L.	6.	monitor	10.	floor plan
3.	S.A.	7.	master control	11.	I.F.B.
4.	intercom	8.	flat		

D. Allows the director to give the talent instructions while the talent is on the air

D ◯ ◯ ◯ ◯
   1   2   3   4
  ◯ ◯ ◯ ◯
   5   6   7   8
  ◯ ◯ ◯
   9 10 11

E. Furniture and other objects used by talent and for set decoration

E ◯ ◯ ◯ ◯
   1   2   3   4
  ◯ ◯ ◯ ◯
   5   6   7   8
  ◯ ◯ ◯
   9 10 11

F. A U-shaped continuous piece of canvas or muslin for backing of scenery and action

F ◯ ◯ ◯ ◯
   1   2   3   4
  ◯ ◯ ◯ ◯
   5   6   7   8
  ◯ ◯ ◯
   9 10 11

G. High-quality video displays used in the studio and control rooms; cannot receive broadcast signals

G ◯ ◯ ◯ ◯
   1   2   3   4
  ◯ ◯ ◯ ◯
   5   6   7   8
  ◯ ◯ ◯
   9 10 11

H. A room adjacent to the studio in which the director, the producer, various production assistants, the TD, the audio engineer, and sometimes the LD perform their various production functions

H ◯ ◯ ◯ ◯
   1   2   3   4
  ◯ ◯ ◯ ◯
   5   6   7   8
  ◯ ◯ ◯
   9 10 11

PAGE TOTAL

I. Controls the program input, storage, and retrieval of on-the-air telecasts; also oversees technical quality of all program material

I ① ② ③ ④
    1   2   3   4
⑤ ⑥ ⑦ ⑧
5   6   7   8
⑨ ⑩ ⑪
9   10   11

J. Major intercommunication device in video production studios

K ① ② ③ ④
    1   2   3   4
⑤ ⑥ ⑦ ⑧
5   6   7   8
⑨ ⑩ ⑪
9   10   11

K. Communication system for all production and engineering personnel involved in the production of a show; includes I.F.B., P.L., S.A., and cellular telephones

L ① ② ③ ④
    1   2   3   4
⑤ ⑥ ⑦ ⑧
5   6   7   8
⑨ ⑩ ⑪
9   10   11

PAGE TOTAL

SECTION TOTAL

REVIEW OF VIDEO PRODUCTION STUDIO AND MAJOR INSTALLATIONS

Select the correct answers and fill in the bubbles with the corresponding numbers.

1. The switcher should be located adjacent to the (12) *LD's* (13) *director's* (14) *producer's* (15) *C.G. operator's* position.

2. The major function of a cyc is to serve as a (16) *sound-deadening device* (17) *continuous background for scenery* (18) *chroma-key area.*

3. You need a separate video monitor (19) *for each video switcher input* (20) *for preset and line video only* (21) *for remote inputs only.*

4. Even for small studios, the minimum ceiling height is (22) *12 feet* (23) *14 feet* (24) *18 feet.*

5. Assuming that the off-the-air receiver (AIR) shows the correct C.G. image, which preview monitors display the wrong picture? *(Multiple answers are possible.)*

(25) *VR-1 monitor*   (32) *C-1 monitor*

(26) *VR-2 monitor*   (33) *C-2 monitor*

(27) *VR-3 monitor*   (34) *C-3 monitor*

(28) *preview monitor*   (35) *line monitor*

(29) *electronic still store monitor* (36) *remote-1 monitor*

(30) *effects monitor*   (37) *remote-2 monitor*

(31) *character generator monitor*

1 ◯ ◯ ◯ ◯
   12 13 14 15

2 ◯   ◯   ◯
   16   17   18

3 ◯   ◯   ◯
   19   20   21

4 ◯   ◯   ◯
   22   23   24

5 ◯ ◯ ◯ ◯ ◯
   25 26 27 28 29
   ◯ ◯ ◯ ◯ ◯
   30 31 32 33 34
   ◯ ◯ ◯
   35 36 37

SECTION TOTAL [   ]

REVIEW OF SCENERY, PROPERTIES, AND SCENIC DESIGN

1. Fill in the bubbles whose numbers correspond with the numbers identifying the various set pieces in the following figure.

38	39	40	41	42	43

a. sweep

b. periaktos

c. pillar

d. square pillar

e. pylon

f. screen

1a ○ 38 ○ 39 ○ 40
     ○ 41 ○ 42 ○ 43

1b ○ 38 ○ 39 ○ 40
     ○ 41 ○ 42 ○ 43

1c ○ 38 ○ 39 ○ 40
     ○ 41 ○ 42 ○ 43

1d ○ 38 ○ 39 ○ 40
     ○ 41 ○ 42 ○ 43

1e ○ 38 ○ 39 ○ 40
     ○ 41 ○ 42 ○ 43

1f ○ 38 ○ 39 ○ 40
     ○ 41 ○ 42 ○ 43

SECTION TOTAL [ ]

2. From the rough floor plans shown below, select the one that most closely matches the simple sets shown on the facing page and fill in the corresponding bubbles. *(Note that there are floor plans that do not match any of the set photos.)*

44

45

46

47

48

49

50

51

52

a.

b.

2a ○ ○ ○ ○ ○
    44 45 46 47 48
    ○ ○ ○ ○
    49 50 51 52

2b ○ ○ ○ ○ ○
    44 45 46 47 48
    ○ ○ ○ ○
    49 50 51 52

c.

d.

2c ○ ○ ○ ○ ○
    44 45 46 47 48
    ○ ○ ○ ○
    49 50 51 52

2d ○ ○ ○ ○ ○
    44 45 46 47 48
    ○ ○ ○ ○
    49 50 51 52

e.

f.

2e ○ ○ ○ ○ ○
    44 45 46 47 48
    ○ ○ ○ ○
    49 50 51 52

2f ○ ○ ○ ○ ○
    44 45 46 47 48
    ○ ○ ○ ○
    49 50 51 52

P A G E
T O T A L [   ]

Select the correct answers and fill in the bubbles with the corresponding numbers.

3. The standard backgrounds used to simulate interior and exterior walls are called (53) *cycs* (54) *flats* (55) *drops.*

4. A bookcase, the books in it, and the chair next to it are all part of (56) *set decoration* (57) *set furniture* (58) *properties.*

5. The usual height for standard set units is (59*)* *7 feet* (60) *10 feet* (61) *14 feet.* For low-ceiling studios, it is (62) *8 feet* (63) *6 feet* (64) *12 feet.* **(Fill in two bubbles.)**

6. To elevate scenery, properties, or action areas, we use (65) *periaktoi* (66) *platforms* (67) *pylons.*

7. Scenic pieces that can be used in a variety of configurations are called (68) *set modules* (69) *hardwall flats* (70) *set dressings.*

8. The painting at the back of an interview set is a (71) *set prop* (72) *hand prop* (73) *set dressing.*

9. A ground row is usually built into the (74) *control room* (75) *hardwall cyc* (76) *prop area.*

10. The desk for the news anchor is considered a (77) *set prop* (78) *hand prop* (79) *set dressing.*

11. The continuous piece of canvas or muslin stretched along two, three, or even all four studio walls to form a uniform background is referred to as (80) *a drop* (81) *canvas backing* (82) *a cyclorama.*

3 ○ 53	○ 54	○ 55
4 ○ 56	○ 57	○ 58
5 ○ 59	○ 60	○ 61
○ 62	○ 63	○ 64
6 ○ 65	○ 66	○ 67
7 ○ 68	○ 69	○ 70
8 ○ 71	○ 72	○ 73
9 ○ 74	○ 75	○ 76
10 ○ 77	○ 78	○ 79
11 ○ 80	○ 81	○ 82

PAGE
TOTAL

SECTION
TOTAL

▊ REVIEW QUIZ

*Mark the following statements as true or false by filling in the bubbles in the **T** (for true) or*
***F** (for false) column.*

		T	F
1.	Lashlines work well for softwall scenery but are not used for hardwall scenery.	**1** ◯ 83	◯ 84
2.	The switcher must be located right next to the producer's position.	**2** ◯ 85	◯ 86
3.	The control room must be equipped with speakers that carry the line-out audio signal.	**3** ◯ 87	◯ 88
4.	The sound control (console) must be located as close to the director as possible.	**4** ◯ 89	◯ 90
5.	A well-functioning S.A. system makes a P.L. unnecessary.	**5** ◯ 91	◯ 92
6.	An accurate control room clock makes the use of a stopwatch unnecessary.	**6** ◯ 93	◯ 94
7.	A monitor is identical to a television set except that it has a sharper picture.	**7** ◯ 95	◯ 96
8.	The program objective has a great influence on the set design.	**8** ◯ 97	◯ 98
9.	In a scenic context, jacks are electrical outlets for prop lamps.	**9** ◯ 99	◯ 100
10.	All active furniture should be placed at least 6 to 8 feet from the background scenery.	**10** ◯ 101	◯ 102
11.	Wagons can be used as platforms.	**11** ◯ 103	◯ 104
12.	A small studio does not need a smooth floor because zoom lenses make dollying unnecessary.	**12** ◯ 105	◯ 106
13.	Most professional production sets, such as a news set, are constructed with hardwall flats.	**13** ◯ 107	◯ 108
14.	The preview (or preset) and line monitors should ideally be side-by-side in the control room.	**14** ◯ 109	◯ 110
15.	In many video productions, props and set dressings are more important than the background flats for indicating a certain style.	**15** ◯ 111	◯ 112

SECTION
TOTAL [   ]

PROBLEM-SOLVING APPLICATIONS

1. You are asked by the new art professor about the feasibility of converting a classroom into a small video production studio. The classroom has no windows, normal doors, a 10-foot ceiling with standard fluorescent lighting, and a wood floor. What would you tell the professor? Be specific.

2. You are asked by the company president why you need so many monitors in the control room. She tells you that she had consulted an electronics engineer, who told her that there are switching devices that let you preview multiple video sources on a single monitor. She quotes the engineer as saying that all you really need are two monitors—a preview and a line monitor. How, if at all, would you defend a multimonitor stack in the control room?

3. You are to evaluate the preliminary design for a new control room (see illustration below). What, if any, changes would you recommend? Why?

4. Using one of the forms at the back of this workbook, draw a floor plan for a weekly interview show dealing with the art and media scene in your city. The host will interview guests from theater, the music scene, radio, and television. Include a detailed prop list.

5. Draw a floor plan for a morning news set. The anchors are a woman and a man, and the news content is geared more toward local gossip than international politics.

15 Production Environment: Field, Postproduction, and Synthetic

REVIEW OF KEY TERMS

Match each term with its appropriate definition by filling in the corresponding bubble.

1. big remote
2. remote truck
3. uplink truck
4. field production

5. contact person
6. EFP
7. remote survey

8. ENG
9. virtual reality
10. synthetic environment

A. Electronically generated settings, either through chroma key or computer

A ① ② ③ ④ ⑤
   1 2 3 4 5
   ⑥ ⑦ ⑧ ⑨ ⑩
   6 7 8 9 10

B. A production of a large, scheduled event outside the studio for live transmission or recorded live

B ① ② ③ ④ ⑤
   1 2 3 4 5
   ⑥ ⑦ ⑧ ⑨ ⑩
   6 7 8 9 10

C. A person who is familiar with and who can facilitate access to the remote location and the key people

C ① ② ③ ④ ⑤
   1 2 3 4 5
   ⑥ ⑦ ⑧ ⑨ ⑩
   6 7 8 9 10

D. Any video production that happens outside the studio

D ① ② ③ ④ ⑤
   1 2 3 4 5
   ⑥ ⑦ ⑧ ⑨ ⑩
   6 7 8 9 10

PAGE TOTAL ☐

1.	big remote	5.	contact person	8.	ENG
2.	remote truck	6.	EFP	9.	virtual reality
3.	uplink truck	7.	remote survey	10.	synthetic environment
4.	field production				

E. Computer-simulated environment with which the user can interact

E ○ ○ ○ ○ ○
   1 2 3 4 5
○ ○ ○ ○ ○
6 7 8 9 10

F. An inspection of the remote location by key production and engineering personnel so that they can plan for the setup and the use of production equipment

F ○ ○ ○ ○ ○
   1 2 3 4 5
○ ○ ○ ○ ○
6 7 8 9 10

G. Small vehicle that sends video and audio signals to a satellite

G ○ ○ ○ ○ ○
   1 2 3 4 5
○ ○ ○ ○ ○
6 7 8 9 10

H. The use of portable camcorders, lights, and sound equipment for the production of unplanned daily news events; usually done for live transmission or immediate postproduction

H ○ ○ ○ ○ ○
   1 2 3 4 5
○ ○ ○ ○ ○
6 7 8 9 10

I. Video production done outside the studio that is usually shot for postproduction (not live)

I ○ ○ ○ ○ ○
   1 2 3 4 5
○ ○ ○ ○ ○
6 7 8 9 10

J. The vehicle that carries the control room, audio control, VR section, video control section, and transmission equipment

J ○ ○ ○ ○ ○
   1 2 3 4 5
○ ○ ○ ○ ○
6 7 8 9 10

PAGE TOTAL

SECTION TOTAL

REVIEW OF ENG AND EFP

Select the correct answers and fill in the bubbles with the corresponding numbers.

1. When interviewing a fire chief on the fire line, your major audio concern is (11) *wind* (12) *ambient sounds* (13) *traffic noise.*

   1 ○ 11 ○ 12 ○ 13

2. Whenever possible you should white-balance your camcorder (14) *every time you enter a new lighting environment* (15) *before going out for a shoot* (16) *only when it gets dark.*

   2 ○ 14 ○ 15 ○ 16

3. The field production least likely to use signal transmission equipment is (17) *ENG* (18) *EFP* (19) *big remotes.*

   3 ○ 17 ○ 18 ○ 19

4. One of the important preproduction activities for EFP is (20) *procuring RCUs for the cameras* (21) *consulting with the art director* (22) *conducting a remote survey.*

   4 ○ 20 ○ 21 ○ 22

5. In EFP the best way to light indoor activities is to (23) *use a few high-powered spotlights* (24) *use several low-powered floodlights* (25) *place the action in front of a window.*

   5 ○ 23 ○ 24 ○ 25

6. When the reporter uses an external hand or lavalier mic, you (26) *should* (27) *should not* open the camera mic simultaneously.

   6 ○ 26 ○ 27

7. A functioning P.L. intercom system is essential for (28) *ENG* (29) *EFP* (30) *big remotes.*

   7 ○ 28 ○ 29 ○ 30

8. The one field production that functions most of the time without a remote survey is (31) *ENG* (32) *EFP* (33) *big remotes.*

   8 ○ 31 ○ 32 ○ 33

9. When using a computer-generated background for live action, you must watch that the (34) *motion vectors* (35) *attached and cast shadows* (36) *colors* match between foreground and background.

   9 ○ 34 ○ 35 ○ 36

10. An equipment checklist is least important for (37) *big remotes* (38) *EFP* (39) *ENG.*

    10 ○ 37 ○ 38 ○ 39

11. When surveying a room for EFP, one of the important items to check is the location of (40) *doors* (41) *ceiling height* (42) *windows.*

    11 ○ 40 ○ 41 ○ 42

PAGE TOTAL ☐

12. Analyze the following survey location sketch and select the major production hazards from the list below. Fill in the bubbles with the corresponding numbers. *(Multiple answers are possible.)*

(43) *little room for cross shooting*

(44) *plants interfering with good composition*

(45) *window causing lighting problems*

(46) *no room for VRs*

(47) *matching color temperatures, if 3,200K fill lights are used*

(48) *computer interfering with video signal*

12 ◯ ◯ ◯
   43 44 45
   ◯ ◯ ◯
   46 47 48

EFP of company president's interview with reporter

Large corner window   Low plant box 18" from floor

South

North

Rubber plant

President

Desk

Reporter

Bookcase

Lamp

Computer

TV set

Live-recording or minimal postproduction
VR Date: 7/15
VR Time: 2:30 pm to 4:30 pm
Place: President's office, Tower Building, 34th floor

PAGE TOTAL

Evaluate the equipment checklists for the three electronic field productions described below.
Identify the **wrong equipment** or **items not needed** to take on-location and fill in the bubbles
with the corresponding numbers. **(Multiple answers are possible.)**

13. Live recording of a brief dance routine in front of city hall.

13 ○ ○ ○ ○ ○
49 50 51 52 53
○ ○ ○ ○
54 55 56 57

CHECKLIST

(49) *3 ENG/EFP cameras*

(50) *6 shotgun mics*

(51) *ESS*

(52) *3 VRs*

(53) *3 RCUs and connecting cables*

(54) *large audio console*

(55) *P.A. audiotape playback system*

(56) *fishpoles for mics*

(57) *C.G.*

14. Live stand-up traffic report from downtown during early-afternoon rush hour.

14 ○ ○ ○ ○ ○
58 59 60 61 62
○ ○ ○ ○
63 64 65 66

CHECKLIST

(58) *digital camcorder*

(59) *2 VRs*

(60) *camera mic*

(61) *hand mic*

(62) *3 portable lighting kits*

(63) *audio recorder*

(64) *microwave transmission equipment*

(65) *I.F.B. intercom*

(66) *C.G.*

15. Video-recorded interview of a media scholar in his hotel room for news item.

15 ○ ○ ○ ○ ○
67 68 69 70 71
○ ○ ○ ○
72 73 74 75

CHECKLIST

(67) *digital camcorder*

(68) *VR*

(69) *portable lighting kit*

(70) *RCU*

(71) *lavalier mic*

(72) *portable audio mixer*

(73) *recording media*

(74) *batteries*

(75) *two preview monitors*

PAGE
TOTAL

SECTION
TOTAL

REVIEW QUIZ

Mark the following statements as true or false by filling in the bubbles in the **T** (for true) or
F (for false) column.

		T	F
1.	A remote truck is usually powered by an external power source.	1 ○ 76	○ 77
2.	There is no difference between a lens-generated and a computer-generated environment.	2 ○ 78	○ 79
3.	If possible, you should do the survey for an outdoor remote during the time the actual production will take place.	3 ○ 80	○ 81
4.	ENG and EFP require the same level of preproduction.	4 ○ 82	○ 83
5.	Contrary to ENG, EFP does not require keeping accurate field logs.	5 ○ 84	○ 85
6.	A satellite uplink truck is essential for transmitting a live ENG pickup from a remote location.	6 ○ 86	○ 87
7.	Keeping an accurate field log is especially important for a live remote pickup.	7 ○ 88	○ 89
8.	Because in EFP the director can check the camera viewfinder, a playback monitor is not necessary.	8 ○ 90	○ 91
9.	A contact person is necessary for EFP and big remotes.	9 ○ 92	○ 93
10.	All synthetic environments must originally be lens-generated.	10 ○ 94	○ 95
11.	A remote survey is important for the technical crew but not the nontechnical people.	11 ○ 96	○ 97
12.	An I.F.B. intercom system is essential for successful EFP.	12 ○ 98	○ 99
13.	A well-equipped remote truck must contain a compact image control center.	13 ○ 100	○ 101
14.	The position of the sun is an important factor in surveys for outdoor remotes.	14 ○ 102	○ 103
15.	Remote surveys are especially important for ENG.	15 ○ 104	○ 105

SECTION TOTAL [ ]

PROBLEM-SOLVING APPLICATIONS

1. To get a good overhead shot of a parade, you would like to place one of the cameras in the twentieth-floor window of a nearby hotel. The TD informs you that the hotel manager has nothing against your renting the room for the day and setting up the camera, but he will not allow any long cable runs either inside or outside the hotel. What would you suggest?

2. To be "on the cutting edge" with his employees, the new company president would like to speak to them from a fantasy landscape yet remain behind his familiar desk. Can you oblige the president's request? If so, how? If not, why not?

3. You are asked to help draw up specifications for a new remote truck for a college broadcasting department that specializes in telecasting all kinds of college sports. What questions should you ask before making a recommendation? Why?

4. The new PA is very upset about your failure to request an adequate P.L. system for the single-camera EFP in the university student union. What would you tell the PA? Why?

5. Conduct a detailed remote survey of two of the following events: a local school board meeting; a rock concert in a city park; a modern dance performance in front of city hall; an interview with a university president in his or her office; the gala opening of a new computer store; a wedding in a local church; a basketball game in a high-school or college gym.

Production Control: Talent and Directing

16 Talent, Clothing, and Makeup

REVIEW OF KEY TERMS

Match each term with its appropriate definition by filling in the corresponding bubble.

1. I.F.B.
2. moiré effect
3. actor
4. performer
5. talent
6. teleprompter
7. blocking
8. foundation
9. cue card

A. Carefully worked-out movement and actions of the talent and all mobile video equipment used in a scene

A ① ② ③ ④ ⑤
     1 2 3 4 5
     ⑥ ⑦ ⑧ ⑨
     6 7 8 9

B. A makeup base, normally done with water-soluble cake makeup

B ① ② ③ ④ ⑤
     1 2 3 4 5
     ⑥ ⑦ ⑧ ⑨
     6 7 8 9

C. A person who appears on-camera in nondramatic shows

C ① ② ③ ④ ⑤
     1 2 3 4 5
     ⑥ ⑦ ⑧ ⑨
     6 7 8 9

D. A prompting system that allows communication with talent while on the air

D ① ② ③ ④ ⑤
     1 2 3 4 5
     ⑥ ⑦ ⑧ ⑨
     6 7 8 9

PAGE TOTAL ☐

1. I.F.B.
2. moiré effect
3. actor

4. performer
5. talent
6. teleprompter

7. blocking
8. foundation
9. cue card

E. Color vibrations that occur when narrow, contrasting stripes of a design interfere with the frequency of the scanning lines of the video system

E ○ ○ ○ ○ ○
   1 2 3 4 5
   ○ ○ ○ ○
   6 7 8 9

F. A large hand-lettered card that contains copy, usually held next to the camera lens by floor personnel

F ○ ○ ○ ○ ○
   1 2 3 4 5
   ○ ○ ○ ○
   6 7 8 9

G. Collective name for all performers and actors who appear regularly on television

G ○ ○ ○ ○ ○
   1 2 3 4 5
   ○ ○ ○ ○
   6 7 8 9

H. A person who appears on-camera in dramatic roles

H ○ ○ ○ ○ ○
   1 2 3 4 5
   ○ ○ ○ ○
   6 7 8 9

I. A device that projects the moving copy over the camera lens so that the talent can read it without losing eye contact with the viewer

I ○ ○ ○ ○ ○
   1 2 3 4 5
   ○ ○ ○ ○
   6 7 8 9

PAGE TOTAL

SECTION TOTAL

REVIEW OF PERFORMANCE TECHNIQUES

1. The following figures show various cues as given to the talent by the floor manager. From the list below, select the specific cue illustrated and fill in the bubble with the corresponding number.

(10) *standby*

(11) *cue*

(12) *on time*

(13) *speed up*

(14) *stretch*

(15) *wind up*

(16) *cut*

(17) *5 minutes left*

(18) *30 seconds left*

(19) *15 seconds left*

a. pulls hands apart

b.

c.

d. rotates hand

1a 10 11 12 13 14 / 15 16 17 18 19

1b 10 11 12 13 14 / 15 16 17 18 19

1c 10 11 12 13 14 / 15 16 17 18 19

1d 10 11 12 13 14 / 15 16 17 18 19

PAGE TOTAL

© 2010 Wadsworth/Cengage

(10) *standby*	(15) *wind up*
(11) *cue*	(16) *cut*
(12) *on time*	(17) *5 minutes left*
(13) *speed up*	(18) *30 seconds left*
(14) *stretch*	(19) *15 seconds left*

e.

f.

g. rotates hand with extended index finger

h. pulls index finger across throat

i.

j.

1e ◯ ◯ ◯ ◯ ◯
  10 11 12 13 14
  ◯ ◯ ◯ ◯ ◯
  15 16 17 18 19

1f ◯ ◯ ◯ ◯ ◯
  10 11 12 13 14
  ◯ ◯ ◯ ◯ ◯
  15 16 17 18 19

1g ◯ ◯ ◯ ◯ ◯
  10 11 12 13 14
  ◯ ◯ ◯ ◯ ◯
  15 16 17 18 19

1h ◯ ◯ ◯ ◯ ◯
  10 11 12 13 14
  ◯ ◯ ◯ ◯ ◯
  15 16 17 18 19

1i ◯ ◯ ◯ ◯ ◯
  10 11 12 13 14
  ◯ ◯ ◯ ◯ ◯
  15 16 17 18 19

1j ◯ ◯ ◯ ◯ ◯
  10 11 12 13 14
  ◯ ◯ ◯ ◯ ◯
  15 16 17 18 19

PAGE TOTAL [ ]

2. The following figures show various cues as given to the talent by the floor manager. From the list below, select the specific cue illustrated and fill in the bubble with the corresponding number.

(20) *VR rolling*

(21) *closer*

(22) *back*

(23) *walk*

(24) *stop*

(25) *OK*

(26) *speak up*

(27) *tone down*

(28) *closer to mic*

(29) *keep talking*

a. fingers open and close like a bird beak

b.

c. pushes palms forward

d.

2a ◯ ◯ ◯ ◯ ◯
     20 21 22 23 24
    ◯ ◯ ◯ ◯ ◯
     25 26 27 28 29

2b ◯ ◯ ◯ ◯ ◯
     20 21 22 23 24
    ◯ ◯ ◯ ◯ ◯
     25 26 27 28 29

2c ◯ ◯ ◯ ◯ ◯
     20 21 22 23 24
    ◯ ◯ ◯ ◯ ◯
     25 26 27 28 29

2d ◯ ◯ ◯ ◯ ◯
     20 21 22 23 24
    ◯ ◯ ◯ ◯ ◯
     25 26 27 28 29

PAGE TOTAL ☐

(20) *VR rolling*		(25) *OK*			
(21) *closer*		(26) *speak up*			
(22) *back*		(27) *tone down*			
(23) *walk*		(28) *closer to mic*			
(24) *stop*		(29) *keep talking*			

e.

f.

g. pulls hands toward body

h. moves fingers back and forth

i.

j.

2e
○ ○ ○ ○ ○
20 21 22 23 24
○ ○ ○ ○ ○
25 26 27 28 29

2f
○ ○ ○ ○ ○
20 21 22 23 24
○ ○ ○ ○ ○
25 26 27 28 29

2g
○ ○ ○ ○ ○
20 21 22 23 24
○ ○ ○ ○ ○
25 26 27 28 29

2h
○ ○ ○ ○ ○
20 21 22 23 24
○ ○ ○ ○ ○
25 26 27 28 29

2i
○ ○ ○ ○ ○
20 21 22 23 24
○ ○ ○ ○ ○
25 26 27 28 29

2j
○ ○ ○ ○ ○
20 21 22 23 24
○ ○ ○ ○ ○
25 26 27 28 29

PAGE
TOTAL

Select the correct answers and fill in the bubbles with the corresponding numbers.

3. When wearing a lavalier mic, you should (30) *maintain your audio level regardless of how far the camera is away from you* (31) *increase your volume when the camera gets farther away from you* (32) *speak more softly when the camera is relatively close to you.*

    3 ○ ○ ○
      30   31   32

4. When asked for an audio level, you should (33) *blow into the mic* (34) *count quickly to five* (35) *recite your opening remarks at on-air levels.*

    4 ○ ○ ○
      33   34   35

5. When you receive cues during the actual video-recording that are different from the rehearsed ones, you should (36) *execute the action as rehearsed* (37) *promptly follow the floor manager's cues* (38) *check with the director.*

    5 ○ ○ ○
      36   37   38

6. From the list below, select the microphone most appropriate for the various performance and acting tasks and fill in the bubbles with the corresponding numbers.

    (39) *desk mics*   (42) *stand mic*

    (40) *hand mic*   (43) *lavalier mic*

    (41) *fishpole mic*

    a. Interview with a celebrity at a busy airport ticket counter.

    6a ○ ○ ○ ○ ○
      39   40   41   42   43

    b. News anchor who remains seated throughout newscast.

    6b ○ ○ ○ ○ ○
      39   40   41   42   43

    c. Moderating a panel discussion with six guests.

    6c ○ ○ ○ ○ ○
      39   40   41   42   43

    d. Lead guitarist of a rock band who also sings and talks to the audience.

    6d ○ ○ ○ ○ ○
      39   40   41   42   43

    e. Two actors doing a brief outdoor scene.

    6e ○ ○ ○ ○ ○
      39   40   41   42   43

7. If you do not use I.F.B. during a studio production, you should take your opening cues from (44) *the camera operator* (45) *the floor manager* (46) *the tally lights.*

    7 ○ ○ ○
      44   45   46

8. For the talent the most accurate indicator of the camera's field of view is (47) *the relative distance between talent and camera* (48) *the floor manager's cues* (49) *the studio monitor.*

    8 ○ ○ ○
      47   48   49

9. When demonstrating a small object, you should (50) *hold it as close to the lens as possible* (51) *keep it as steady as possible or on the display table* (52) *move it slowly toward the camera.*

    9 ○ ○ ○
      50   51   52

PAGE TOTAL [   ]

SECTION TOTAL [   ]

10. Read the following copy into a mirror or video camera or, ideally, into a television camera with a teleprompter at least three times. Video-record your performances. Time your narration with a stopwatch and try to match your times with the ones given in subsequent readings.

a. news copy

```
Package: Australia Earth Mover

TALENT O/C          IN SOUTHERN AUSTRALIA,
(ON CAMERA)         ENGINEERS ARE RAVING ABOUT A NEW
                    DEVELOPMENT...A GIANT EARTH MOVER
                    THAT HAS NO WHEELS. CHIEF ENGINEER
                    FRED STEINER SAYS HE OBSERVED HOW A
                    CENTIPEDE TRAVELS AND SIMPLY COPIED
                    ITS MOVEMENTS.


SERVER FILE
0120
VO                  THE MANY LEGS ENABLE THE MACHINE TO
                    NEGOTIATE DITCHES, BUSHES, AND EVEN
                    GOOD-SIZED BOULDERS WITHOUT SPILLING
                    ITS LOAD OR TIPPING OVER.

                    JOHN HEWITT TALKED TO THE DRIVER...OR
                    RIDER?...OF THE MONSTER CENTIPEDE...


SERVER FILE
0121
SOS
(SOUND ON SOURCE)
1:45
```

Given time: 29 seconds

Your first reading: _____ seconds

Your second reading: _____ seconds

Your third reading: _____ seconds

b. introduction to a weekly sports show

```
VIDEO               AUDIO

STANDARD
OPENING
SERVER FILE
SP 772


WALTER O/C          Hi, I'm Alex Walter. Welcome
                    to Sports at Four. Today we have
                    with us the world's most prominent
                    and amazing mountain climber--


CU MESSNER          Reinhold Messner. He will talk to us
                    about how he prepared for his extreme
                    climbs and what he thought and felt
C.G.: EVEREST       when he climbed--often alone--the big
                    walls of the world's highest peaks.


WALTER O/C          He has brought with him some of the
                    best mountain-climbing footage I have
                    ever seen--and he will share it with
                    us. We will also see where Reinhold
                    lives and what he does now. All coming
                    up next on Sports at Four.

-----------------------------------------------------------
SERVER FILE         COMMERCIAL #1
SP 844
-----------------------------------------------------------
```

Given time: 35 seconds

Your first reading: _____ seconds

Your second reading: _____ seconds

Your third reading: _____ seconds

c. commercial *(Note that this commercial represents a high-pressure pitch and requires fast reading.)*

```
VIDEO                 AUDIO

CHROMA KEY
ESS 64: CARS

CU OF BAKER           Hi, I'm Tom Baker of Baker Chevrolet
ZOOM OUT TO MS        to talk to you about automobile
                      leasing. It can mean lower monthly
                      payments, and it lets you keep that
                      down payment for other things you
                      need.

CUT TO C.G.:
LOWER MONTHLY
PAYMENTS

CUT TO                For example, you can lease this
ESS 65: CAR 1         brand-new beauty for only 300 dollars
ESS 66: CAR 2         per month or this fuel-efficient
                      luxury car for only 499 dollars per
                      month--and we'll even buy your old
                      car and give you the cash!

CUT TO                So come on down and drive away
CU OF BAKER +         your dream car.
CHROMA KEY ESS 64

CUT TO C.G.           It's only at Baker Chevrolet in
SIGNATURE             Virginia City. Come in right now
                      and save!
```

Given time: 30 seconds

Your first reading: _____ seconds

Your second reading: _____ seconds

Your third reading: _____ seconds

REVIEW OF PERFORMANCE AND ACTING TECHNIQUES

Select the correct answers and fill in the bubbles with the corresponding numbers.

1. To keep eye contact with the viewer when cameras are switched on you, you need to (53) *follow the tally lights* (54) *follow the floor manager's cues* (55) *listen to the producer's I.F.B. cues.*

   1 ◯ 53 ◯ 54 ◯ 55

2. To establish eye contact with the viewer, you need to pretend to (56) *look through the lens* (57) *converse with the floor manager* (58) *converse with the camera operator.*

   2 ◯ 56 ◯ 57 ◯ 58

3. When you receive the floor manager's time cue, you should (59) *give the floor manager a brief nod to acknowledge the cue* (60) *verify it by glancing at the clock* (61) *do nothing but adjust your performance to the remaining time.*

   3 ◯ 59 ◯ 60 ◯ 61

4. When you can't see the teleprompter well enough, you should (62) *have the camera move closer to you* (63) *ask the operator to slow down the scroll* (64) *have the font made bigger.*

   4 ◯ 62 ◯ 63 ◯ 64

5. When doing an O/S or cross-shooting scene, you must adjust your blocking so that you see (65) *the key light* (66) *the floor manager* (67) *the camera lens.*

   5 ◯ 65 ◯ 66 ◯ 67

6. When substituting for the regular host of a studio talk show for the first time, you should (68) *discuss the lighting with the LD* (69) *verify the specific cues with the floor manager* (70) *test the quality of the microphone used.*

   6 ◯ 68 ◯ 69 ◯ 70

7. Pretend that you (person A) are receiving a telephone call from person B. In this scene we see and hear only A (you) but not B. Using exactly the same dialogue (see the script on the following page), adapt your delivery and acting style to at least two of the following circumstances:

   a. B calls to tell you that she had her first novel published.

   b. B has quit her job.

   c. B has just wrecked your new car.

   d. B has called off the wedding.

   e. B has won big in the lottery.

   f. B has been arrested.

   g. B has lost her job.

   h. B has won an Emmy for innovative productions.

   Place the scene anywhere you like. You may do well to write the other part of the phone conversation so that you can listen and respond more convincingly.

   SECTION TOTAL [   ]

PHONE CONVERSATION
Hello?
Hi.
Fine, and you?
Good.
No.
No, really. It's always a good time when you call.
I beg your pardon?
You must be kidding.
Yes.
No.
What does Chris say to all this?
No. Should I?
I don't know.
Perhaps.
You want me to come over now?
Yes. Really.
Well, this changes things somewhat.
I think so.
I'm not so sure.
Yes. No. I...
All right. But not...
OK.
If you think this is...
Definitely.
Good-bye...When?
No. Really.
Good-bye.

REVIEW OF CLOTHING AND MAKEUP

Select the correct answers and fill in the bubbles with the corresponding numbers.

1. One of the most widely used makeup foundations is (71) *water-based cake* (72) *grease base* (73) *oil-based foundation.*

   1 ◯ ◯ ◯
      71   72   73

2. During a green-backdrop chroma key, you should not wear (74) *red* (75) *blue* (76) *green* because this color will let the background show through during the key.

   2 ◯ ◯ ◯
      74   75   76

3. The dress of a pop singer has many rhinestones that sparkle under the colored stage lights. This dress is (77) *acceptable* (78) *unacceptable* because (79) *the digital camera can handle small areas of extreme bright light* (80) *there is too much brightness contrast* (81) *it will result in moiré patterns* (82) *it will reinforce the stage lighting.* **(Fill in two bubbles.)**

   3 ◯ ◯
      77   78
   ◯ ◯ ◯ ◯
   79 80 81 82

4. When doing makeup, you should have lighting conditions that are the same as or close to those of (83) *your customary makeup room* (84) *the actual production environment* (85) *normal 3,200K studio lights.*

   4 ◯ ◯ ◯
      83   84   85

5. Clothing with thin, highly contrasting stripes or checkered patterns is (86) *acceptable* (87) *not acceptable* because (88) *the CCD camera can handle such a contrast quite easily* (89) *it provides exciting patterns* (90) *it results in moiré color vibrations* (91) *it is too detailed for the camera to see.* **(Fill in two bubbles.)**

   5 ◯ ◯
      86   87
   ◯ ◯ ◯ ◯
   88 89 90 91

SECTION TOTAL [ ]

*Mark the following statements as true or false by filling in the bubbles in the **T** (for true) or*
***F** (for false) column.*

		T	F
1.	A close-up speeds up all movements.	**1** ○ 92	○ 93
2.	When working with a teleprompter, it is best to move the camera as close as possible to the talent.	**2** ○ 94	○ 95
3.	In a cross shot, you should stand on your mark even if you can't see the camera lens.	**3** ○ 96	○ 97
4.	Because you never know what you will be asked to read in an audition, you should not prepare for it but can and should rely on the energy of the moment.	**4** ○ 98	○ 99
5.	You can ignore the time cues by the floor manager so long as you can see the studio clock.	**5** ○ 100	○ 101
6.	When on a close-up, you need to keep your actions tighter and slower than normal.	**6** ○ 102	○ 103
7.	You should try to get the floor manager's attention when you think that you should have received a time cue.	**7** ○ 104	○ 105
8.	Because of possible moiré effects, you should avoid wearing high-contrast striped patterns on-camera.	**8** ○ 106	○ 107
9.	In contrast to television performers, actors always portray someone else.	**9** ○ 108	○ 109
10.	If you discover that you are talking to the wrong camera, you should look down and then look up into the on-the-air camera.	**10** ○ 110	○ 111
11.	What you wear is really unimportant when simply auditioning for a role.	**11** ○ 112	○ 113
12.	The best way to give an audio level is to quickly count to five.	**12** ○ 114	○ 115
13.	The term *talent* refers to both actors and performers.	**13** ○ 116	○ 117
14.	A "cut" cue from the floor manager means that the director is cutting (switching) to the next camera.	**14** ○ 118	○ 119

SECTION
TOTAL

PROBLEM-SOLVING APPLICATIONS

1. The interviewer for the new weekly *Blues Review* show arrives in a bright red dress. She will interview the songwriter in the dimly lit backstage area of the opera house. Although the camera operator is using a small three-chip digital camcorder, he is somewhat concerned about the interviewer's attire. Why? What would you suggest?

2. The ENG camera operator is concerned about proper fill light for you, the reporter, during a live transmission of a traffic report on the fog-shrouded Golden Gate Bridge, so he asks for an additional person to handle the fill light. Do you share the camera operator's concern? If so, why? If not, why not?

3. The ENG camera operator suggests that you do your stand-up report right in front of the bright, sunlit wall of city hall. According to the camera operator, the automatic-iris control would guarantee a high-key lighting effect which, in turn, would reflect the upbeat story you have to tell. Do you agree with the camera operator? If so, why? If not, why not?

4. To practice blocking, write down a series of moves that carry you around your kitchen. For example, you can start at the stove, then get the teakettle out of the cupboard, put it on the stove, go back to pick up the telephone, put down the telephone to answer the door, and so forth. Try to hit the same marks each time you go through the routine. If possible, have a friend video-record your blocking maneuvers from the same camera position. You can then compare the recordings and check how accurate your blocking was. As part of the same exercise, you can use various props (kitchen utensils) and see how the camera's field of view (LS to ECU) will influence your handling of props.

5. Do your favorite monologue and video-record it (or, better, have someone else record it) first in a loose medium shot, then in a CU, and finally in an ECU. Analyze how the camera's field of view changes (or should change) your delivery and try to adjust your acting to each circumstance. Note especially the relative speed of your delivery and your facial expressions.

17 Putting It All Together: Directing

Match each term with its appropriate definition by filling in the corresponding bubble.

1. **dry run**
2. **time line**
3. **visualization**
4. **walk-through/camera rehearsal**
5. **angle**
6. **single-column drama script**
7. **two-column A/V script**
8. **shot**
9. **camera rehearsal**
10. **blocking**
11. **multicamera directing**
12. **single-camera directing**
13. **fact sheet**
14. **take**

A. A combination orientation session and follow-up run-through with equipment

A ① ② ③ ④ ⑤
   ⑥ ⑦ ⑧ ⑨ ⑩
   ⑪ ⑫ ⑬ ⑭

B. Traditional television script format with both audio and video information

B ① ② ③ ④ ⑤
   ⑥ ⑦ ⑧ ⑨ ⑩
   ⑪ ⑫ ⑬ ⑭

C. Determining the positions and the actions of talent and equipment

C ① ② ③ ④ ⑤
   ⑥ ⑦ ⑧ ⑨ ⑩
   ⑪ ⑫ ⑬ ⑭

PAGE TOTAL ☐

1. dry run	5. angle	10. blocking
2. time line	6. single-column drama script	11. multicamera directing
3. visualization	7. two-column A/V script	12. single-camera directing
4. walk-through/camera rehearsal	8. shot	13. fact sheet
	9. camera rehearsal	14. take

D. The schedule of a production day

D
○ ○ ○ ○ ○
1　2　3　4　5
○ ○ ○ ○ ○
6　7　8　9　10
○ ○ ○ ○
11　12　13　14

E. Same as dress rehearsal

E
○ ○ ○ ○ ○
1　2　3　4　5
○ ○ ○ ○ ○
6　7　8　9　10
○ ○ ○ ○
11　12　13　14

F. Coordinating the simultaneous use of several cameras from the control room

F
○ ○ ○ ○ ○
1　2　3　4　5
○ ○ ○ ○ ○
6　7　8　9　10
○ ○ ○ ○
11　12　13　14

G. The basic approach to a story

G
○ ○ ○ ○ ○
1　2　3　4　5
○ ○ ○ ○ ○
6　7　8　9　10
○ ○ ○ ○
11　12　13　14

H. Rehearsal without equipment

H
○ ○ ○ ○ ○
1　2　3　4　5
○ ○ ○ ○ ○
6　7　8　9　10
○ ○ ○ ○
11　12　13　14

PAGE TOTAL ☐

I. Traditional script format for television plays

J. A list of features the talent should mention on-camera when demonstrating a product

K. The mental image of a shot

L. Guiding the use of a single camcorder for video-recording scripted events for postproduction

M. The interval between two transitions

N. Any one of similar repeated shots taken during video recording or filming

REVIEW OF VISUALIZATION, CONTEXT, AND SEQUENCING

1. The following sketches show visualizations that change with different contexts. Fill in the bubbles that most closely match each visualization with its most appropriate context.

Set 1:

| 15 | 16 | 17 |

   a. This dog food is rich in vitamins.

   b. Danger! This might be a bomb!

   c. This can looks old—let's throw it away.

Set 2:

| 18 | 19 | 20 |

   d. As a luxury car, it is in a class by itself.

   e. It handles like a sports car.

   f. It has a powerful engine.

1a	○ 15	○ 16	○ 17
1b	○ 15	○ 16	○ 17
1c	○ 15	○ 16	○ 17
1d	○ 18	○ 19	○ 20
1e	○ 18	○ 19	○ 20
1f	○ 18	○ 19	○ 20

SECTION TOTAL [ ]

REVIEW OF INTERPRETING STORYBOARDS

1. Each of the following four storyboards shows one or several major problems. Fill in the bubbles whose numbers correspond with one or more of these major problems: (21) *poor continuity and disturbance of the mental map* (22) *wrong field-of-view designation* (23) *wrong above- or below-eye-level camera position.* **(Note: Storyboards may exhibit more than one problem.)**

Storyboard a Man and woman looking at each other

CU of woman   Cut to: CU of man   Cut to: 2-shot   Cut to: Tighter 2-shot

1a ○ 21 ○ 22 ○ 23

Storyboard b Runner finishing in first place

CU of runner   Cut to: LS of runner   Cut to: MS of runner   Diss. to: ECU of runner at finish

1b ○ 21 ○ 22 ○ 23

Storyboard c Teacher talking to girl

Knee-shot of girl   Cut to: MCU of teacher   Cut to: Tight 2-shot   Cut to: LS of teacher (profile)

1c ○ 21 ○ 22 ○ 23

Storyboard d Rock star talking to fan

2-shot of man and boy   Cut to: CU of man   Cut to: CU of boy   Cut to: Low-angle shot of boy

1d ○ 21 ○ 22 ○ 23

SECTION TOTAL

© 2010 Wadsworth/Cengage

REVIEW OF SCRIPT MARKING

1. Match each field-of-view designation with its appropriate full term by filling in the bubble with the corresponding number.

(24) *cross-shot*   (26) *long shot*   (29) *extreme long shot*
(25) *over-the-shoulder*   (27) *extreme close-up*   (30) *close-up*
     shot   (28) *medium shot*

a. CU

b. MS

c. O/S

d. X/S

e. ECU

f. LS

g. ELS

1a ○ ○ ○ ○
   24 25 26 27
   ○ ○ ○
   28 29 30

1b ○ ○ ○ ○
   24 25 26 27
   ○ ○ ○
   28 29 30

1c ○ ○ ○ ○
   24 25 26 27
   ○ ○ ○
   28 29 30

1d ○ ○ ○ ○
   24 25 26 27
   ○ ○ ○
   28 29 30

1e ○ ○ ○ ○
   24 25 26 27
   ○ ○ ○
   28 29 30

1f ○ ○ ○ ○
   24 25 26 27
   ○ ○ ○
   28 29 30

1g ○ ○ ○ ○
   24 25 26 27
   ○ ○ ○
   28 29 30

PAGE
TOTAL

Select the correct answers and fill in the bubbles with the corresponding numbers.

2. The script markings in the following figure are (31) *acceptable* (32) *unacceptable* because they (33) *are too small* (34) *have unnecessary or redundant cues* (35) *are in the wrong place* (36) *show large, essential cues.* **(Fill in two bubbles.)**

2   ○   ○
      31   32

○   ○   ○   ○
33   34   35   36

JOHN

What's the matter?   *Ready camera 1*
                             Ready to cue Tammy

TAMMY

                             Cue Tammy and
Nothing.   *take camera 1*

JOHN

What do you mean, "nothing"? I can feel something is wrong.

TAMMY   *Ready to cue John*
                 Ready to take camera 2

Well, I am glad you have some feeling left.

JOHN   *Cue John and take*
         camera 2

What's that supposed to mean?

TAMMY

Please, let's not start that again.

JOHN

Start what again?

TAMMY   *Ready to take camera 3*
                 for a two-shot
Well, I guess it's time to talk.   *Take camera 3*

JOHN

What do you think we have been doing all this time?

PAGE TOTAL [ ]

SECTION TOTAL [ ]

REVIEW OF DIRECTOR'S TERMINOLOGY

1. From the list below, select the director's visualization cue necessary to adjust the picture on the left screen to the picture on the right screen (in pairs from a through l) and fill in the bubbles with the corresponding numbers.

(37) *tilt up*
(38) *tilt down*
(39) *dolly in*
(40) *dolly out*
(41) *zoom in*

(42) *zoom out*
(43) *truck right*
(44) *arc left*
(45) *pedestal down or crane down*

(46) *pedestal up or crane up*
(47) *pan left*
(48) *pan right*

a.

1a ○ 37 ○ 38 ○ 39 ○ 40
    ○ 41 ○ 42 ○ 43 ○ 44
    ○ 45 ○ 46 ○ 47 ○ 48

b.

1b ○ 37 ○ 38 ○ 39 ○ 40
    ○ 41 ○ 42 ○ 43 ○ 44
    ○ 45 ○ 46 ○ 47 ○ 48

c.

1c ○ 37 ○ 38 ○ 39 ○ 40
    ○ 41 ○ 42 ○ 43 ○ 44
    ○ 45 ○ 46 ○ 47 ○ 48

PAGE TOTAL

d.

1d

○ 37	○ 38	○ 39	○ 40
○ 41	○ 42	○ 43	○ 44
○ 45	○ 46	○ 47	○ 48

e.

1e

○ 37	○ 38	○ 39	○ 40
○ 41	○ 42	○ 43	○ 44
○ 45	○ 46	○ 47	○ 48

f.

1f

○ 37	○ 38	○ 39	○ 40
○ 41	○ 42	○ 43	○ 44
○ 45	○ 46	○ 47	○ 48

g.

1g

○ 37	○ 38	○ 39	○ 40
○ 41	○ 42	○ 43	○ 44
○ 45	○ 46	○ 47	○ 48

h.

1h

○ 37	○ 38	○ 39	○ 40
○ 41	○ 42	○ 43	○ 44
○ 45	○ 46	○ 47	○ 48

P A G E
T O T A L [   ]

(37)	tilt up	(42)	zoom out	(46)	pedestal up
(38)	tilt down	(43)	truck right		or crane up
(39)	dolly in	(44)	arc left	(47)	pan left
(40)	dolly out	(45)	pedestal down	(48)	pan right
(41)	zoom in		or crane down		

i.

1i
○ 37	○ 38	○ 39	○ 40
○ 41	○ 42	○ 43	○ 44
○ 45	○ 46	○ 47	○ 48

j.

1j
○ 37	○ 38	○ 39	○ 40
○ 41	○ 42	○ 43	○ 44
○ 45	○ 46	○ 47	○ 48

k.

1k
○ 37	○ 38	○ 39	○ 40
○ 41	○ 42	○ 43	○ 44
○ 45	○ 46	○ 47	○ 48

l.

1l
○ 37	○ 38	○ 39	○ 40
○ 41	○ 42	○ 43	○ 44
○ 45	○ 46	○ 47	○ 48

PAGE TOTAL [ ]

2. From the list below, select the correct director's switching cues by filling in the corresponding bubbles. *(Multiple answers are possible.)*

2 ○ ○ ○
   49 50 51
○ ○ ○
52 53 54

(49) *Ready to take camera two. Take camera two.*
(50) *Ready three. Take three.*
(51) *Ready one. Dissolve to one.*
(52) *Ready to go to black. Go to black.*
(53) *Ready wipe. Dissolve to two.*
(54) *Ready to change C.G. page. Change page.*

3. From the list below, select the correct director's cues to the floor manager by filling in the corresponding bubbles. *(The talent consists of two men and two women. Multiple answers are possible.)*

3 ○ ○ ○
   55 56 57
○ ○ ○
58 59 60

(55) *Ready to cue Mary. Cue Mary.*
(56) *Ready to cue him. Cue him.*
(57) *Make him talk faster.*
(58) *Move her stage-right.*
(59) *Turn the can counterclockwise.*
(60) *Have two of them come closer to the camera.*

4. From the list below, select the director who uses the correct sequence of cues for the opening of a two-camera (C1 and C2) interview and fill in the corresponding bubble. *(There is a title key for the guest. Assume that the crew has received a general standby cue and that bars and tone have already been recorded on the tape by the AD.)*

4 ○ ○ ○
   61 62 63

(61) *Director A:* "Ready to take C.G. Slate. Take slate. Ready black. Black. Beeper. Ready to come up on one CU of host—take one. Cue host. Ready two [on guest]. Take two. Cue guest. Key title. Take one."

(62) *Director B:* "Ready to roll VTR. Roll VTR. Ready C.G. Slate. Read slate. Ready black. Ready beeper. To black. Beeper. Ready to come up on one. Key. Up on one. Ready two. Take two. Lose key. Ready one. Take one."

(63) *Director C:* "Ready to roll VTR. Roll VTR. Ready C.G. Slate. Take C.G. Read slate. Ready black. Ready beeper. To black. Beeper. One, CU of host. Ready to come up on one. Open mic, cue host, up on one. Two, CU of guest. Ready two. Ready to key C.G. Take two, key. Lose key. Ready one, two-shot. Take one."

PAGE TOTAL

SECTION TOTAL

REVIEW OF REHEARSAL TECHNIQUES

Select the correct answers and fill in the bubbles with the corresponding numbers.

1. If pressed for time, you should call for (64) *an uninterrupted camera rehearsal* (65) *a blocking rehearsal* (66) *a walk-through/camera rehearsal.*

   1 ○ ○ ○
   64 65 66

2. Rehearsals that combine walk-throughs and camera rehearsal are most efficiently conducted from the (67) *studio floor* (68) *rehearsal hall* (69) *control room.*

   2 ○ ○ ○
   67 68 69

3. When engaged in EFP, you need not worry about (70) *talent and technical walk-throughs* (71) *cross-overs from one location to the next* (72) *the various camera positions.*

   3 ○ ○ ○
   70 71 72

4. Blocking rehearsals are most efficiently conducted (73) *from the control room* (74) *on the studio floor or in a rehearsal hall* (75) *on the actual studio set.*

   4 ○ ○ ○
   73 74 75

5. Camera rehearsal is conducted (76) *similarly to a dress rehearsal* (77) *for cameras only* (78) *for all technical operations but without talent.*

   5 ○ ○ ○
   76 77 78

SECTION TOTAL

REVIEW QUIZ

*Mark the following statements as true or false by filling in the bubbles in the **T** (for true) or
F (for false) column.*

		T	F
1.	A good floor plan will greatly facilitate camera and talent blocking.	**1** ○ 79	○ 80
2.	If the script marking simply indicates "②" for the shot that is on the air and "③" for the next, it implies that you should give a "Ready three" cue and then call for a "Take three."	**2** ○ 81	○ 82
3.	Proper visualization is essential for correct sequencing.	**3** ○ 83	○ 84
4.	Because the director is engaged in artistic activities, knowledge of the technical production aspects is relatively unimportant.	**4** ○ 85	○ 86
5.	When marking a script, the ready cues must be written in just before the actual take cues.	**5** ○ 87	○ 88
6.	Although the program objective is important to the director in the production phase, it is relatively unimportant in preproduction.	**6** ○ 89	○ 90
7.	When directing a daily newscast, you do not need a floor plan to preplan the camera shots.	**7** ○ 91	○ 92
8.	When doing an EFP, uninterrupted camera rehearsals are more important than when doing a studio show.	**8** ○ 93	○ 94
9.	The "notes" activity during a production requires scheduled time for the corresponding "reset."	**9** ○ 95	○ 96
10.	During a walk-through/camera rehearsal, the director rehearses primarily from the studio floor.	**10** ○ 97	○ 98

SECTION TOTAL

PROBLEM-SOLVING APPLICATIONS

1. When asked to direct an on-location television adaptation of the current theater arts department stage play in the local park, you are advised by the theater director of the play that he will determine the number and the positions of the cameras because he, after all, knows the stage blocking better than you do. What is your reaction? What would you suggest?

2. You are to determine on-camera shots and mark a script for an involved scene of a three-camera, live-recorded situation comedy. The producer tells you that all she can give you is the script, not the complete floor plan. Because of a computer failure, the art director cannot transfer his rough sketch into a finished floor plan, and there is no way to get it to you before rehearsal. Can you proceed with your preproduction activities? If so, how? If not, why not?

3. When you're directing an EFP of a documentary segment on the lumber industry, the producer tells you not to worry too much about shot continuity because he intends to put the show together in extensive postproduction editing. Do you agree with the producer? If so, why? If not, why not?

4. During the evening news, the wrong story comes up on the server monitor. What can you do?

5. During an O/S sequence in a multicamera dramatic production, one of the actors has trouble hitting the blocking marks and is frequently obscured by the camera-near person. What advice would you give the actor?

Scale: ¼" = 1'

Scale: ¼" = 1'

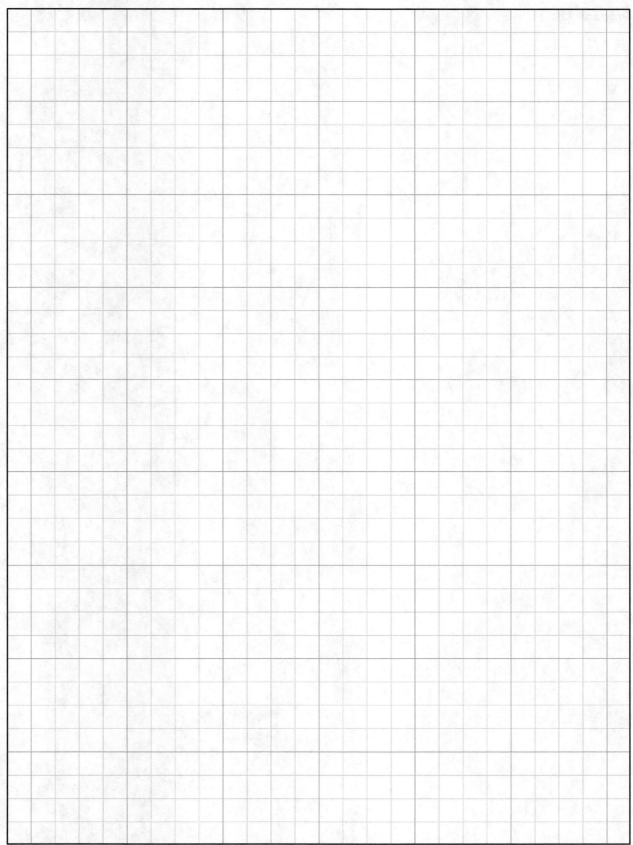

Scale: ¼" = 1'

Property List